Life with Forty Dogs

MISADVENTURES WITH RUNTS, REJECTS, RETIREES, AND RESCUES

JOSEPH ROBERTIA

ALASKA
NORTHWEST
BOOKS®

To Colleen,
for always understanding so much.

Library of Congress Cataloging-in-Publication Data
Names: Robertia, Joseph.
Title: Life with forty dogs : a memoir of Alaskan misadventures /
Joseph Robertia.
Description: Portland, Oregon : Alaska Northwest Books, 2017.
Identifiers: LCCN 2016034187 (print) | LCCN 2016059900 (ebook)
| ISBN 9781943328918 (pbk.) | ISBN 9781943328925 (ebook)
Subjects: LCSH: Sled dogs—Alaska—Anecdotes. | Sled dog
racing—Alaska—Anecdotes. | Robertia, Joseph.
Classification: LCC SF428.7 .R63 2017 (print) | LCC SF428.7 (ebook) |
DDC 636.73—dc23
LC record available at https://lccn.loc.gov/2016034187

Designed by Vicki Knapton

Published by Alaska Northwest Books®
An imprint of

GRAPHIC ARTS
BOOKS®

www.graphicartsbooks.com

"A bone to the dog is not charity.
Charity is the bone shared with the dog,
when you are just as hungry as the dog."

—JACK LONDON

Contents

Acknowledgments

WRITING A FIRST BOOK HAS A LOT OF PARALLELS TO BEING a freshly whelped pup. You've spent months cramped in the same position in a tiny space; so much time has passed that when you see the sun, you squint at the light when taking those first few steps outside; and initially you're completely unclear about what is going on and how to fulfill your role in it all. Because of this, I'm indebted to several people for making this process possible, or at the very least, more palatable.

The idea for this book was born when my father-in-law, Bill Morrow—after hearing so many of our misadventures and delighting in them—suggested that I compile a few into a collection for others to read and enjoy. He wasn't the first person to say I should write a book, but he was the first to truly mean it, and I will always owe him for that.

I am equally indebted to his wife, Rusty, who after I had made the decision to lay down a few stories and began pedaling them, encouraged me to find literary professionals and a publishing house that believed in my work as much as I did. I have to thank Doug Pfeiffer and Jennifer Newens, the publishing directors at Graphic Arts Books for being those people and that publisher. Editor Kathy Howard, designer Vicki Knapton, and marketer Angie Zbornik also added to my success.

I have to thank Dean Osmar and Sarah Armstrong for hiring my wife as a handler, where for three years she learned the basics of mushing. Dean never took it easy on her, or me, when we first started running dogs with him, but we became better mushers because of his tough love teaching style. Also, despite being an Iditarod champion, Dean always treated us like equals, then and now.

Mitch Michaud and Jane Fuerstenau deserve a nod for also getting us into sled dogs through their public outreach while presiding over the Peninsula Sled Dog and Racing Association, and helping us build and constantly fix sleds we battered.

I am equally indebted to Kevin and Deb Hayes, Thera and Emma Mullet, and many other family and friends who gave Lynx attention, helped with dog chores, brought by meals, or offered simple support whenever I needed to work on this book or meet a looming deadline. Jim Frates of the Kenai Peninsula Food Bank also has, for years, aided our kennel by alerting us when large quantities of freezer-burned salmon and other meat were available for donation. These added rations meant far fewer drives north to Anchorage for dog food, which provided me more time to write, and had the added benefit of always making tails wag when these meals were offered in addition to the regular kibble.

My father, Joe Robertia Sr., deserves recognition too, for planting in me as a child the seeds of literary love that eventually grew to fruition in the form of becoming a freelance writer, and now author. Exhausted from the heavy demands of being a true blue-collar workingman, my dad somehow always rallied enough energy to take me to the comic shop, local bookstore, or library instead of just plopping me in front of a TV.

I am very appreciative of the editing efforts of Monica Mullet, Emma Mullet, Travis Wright, Amanda Burg, Kyle Ferguson, Kim Morgan, Ray Lee, and other witty members of my local writing group: The Kenai Peninsula Finer Things Club. Dave Atcheson also gets credit for giving me some writing tips and answering many of my questions about navigating the long and twisty trail to finding a publisher.

My wife, Colleen, deserves the lead dog's share of credit for this book, for not only passing on so much of her mushing knowledge to me, but for always being a partner in this unorthodox lifestyle. Living with forty dogs has never been easy, but from the abysmal lows to the Everest highs, the cumulative experience has been an unforgettable journey, and one I'm glad we endeavored together. I simply couldn't have survived it without such a physically and emotionally strong woman, and she's the only one I want by my side. Cole also read and edited countless drafts of all these stories, and stalwartly encouraged me to never give up on believing this book would eventually see the light of day.

I'm also obliged to my daughter, Lynx, the littlest pup in our pack, for continually reinspiring me with her own love of nature, flair with all animals, and ability to enthusiastically roll with a lifestyle revolving around so many dogs and dog-related chores.

Unquestionably though, I am most grateful to our dogs, for all the adventures we've shared, for showing me so much amazing country I wouldn't have seen without them, and for inspiring me to write this book and, even before that, for revealing to me that I had a story to tell— their story.

Introduction

ALASKA—UNTAMED, UNRESTRAINED, THE EDGE OF THE WILD. It's been said this Last Frontier is made up of people who don't fit in but fit here better than anywhere else. I can't speak for everyone, but this maxim certainly resonated with my wife, Colleen, and me. In the Lower 48 we always sensed something was wrong. Not with us, but with everyone else. The get-ahead materialism, the I-need-more consumerism; we believed life was about doing—and being—so much more. We felt a calling, a hunger not satiated in a world addicted to lattes and laptops, governed by traffic and time clocks, and constructed of concrete and steel. This mutual feeling brought us north in search of something, but to what, we didn't know at the time.

Where we'd settle remained undetermined, as was how long we would stay, or what we would do for income. We only knew we were drawn by a deep aspiration to live a more purposeful life, closer to nature, and filled with adventure. In a stroke of serendipity, the first place we secured was a stamp-sized cabin with no running water in a tiny town called Kasilof. Little did we know, the area we moved to—and have since called home—was a mushing mecca.

Soon after settling in, we discovered teams of sled dogs blew by several times a day—their paws churning up the fresh powder, their pink tongues dangling, and hot breath billowing into the cold air. We quickly learned that within three square miles of our new home lived half a dozen mushers, cumulatively owning more than 300 huskies between them. Sitting on our porch at dusk, the wails washing over us were more than a wave of sound; we felt flooded by the tidal surge of full-throated howls from the various dog packs.

As lifelong animal lovers, we were immediately awestruck by the camaraderie between human and dog pack, intrigued by the joy of purpose they both seemed to share, and inspired to learn more. Within a few months we were apprenticing under other mushers and had gotten our first few sled dogs, primarily rogues, runts, and rejects from other kennels, as well as several pups from local shelters. We've never bought a single one, and initially we got what we paid for. They were a motley bunch of untrained and nearly uncontrollable hyperactive huskies. We had no leaders and to gain any kind of forward momentum, one of us had to run down the trail in front of the raucous mob.

But, over time, they learned. Leaders emerged, their conditioning improved, and a team coalesced. Within a few years we consistently had forty dogs living with us (and a high of forty-five at our peak, before a few old-timers passed on). Vacations ended and the bank account drained as every penny we had went to specially formulated kibble, veterinary care, and inordinate amounts of cold weather gear and mushing equipment. Every moment we weren't at work we spent in the company of our huskies.

We forged the life we longed for, one spent almost entirely outdoors and that moved with the rhythm of the seasons—a simple life, but far from easy. In spring, we tilled the soil and sowed a garden, as well as felled trees, cut the logs into rounds, and stacked the lumber to feed our woodstove when the weather turned cold. In summer we turned to the sea, setting gillnets to snare salmon, stocking chest freezers full with the silver slabs that we and the dogs dined on as our major source of protein. Fall was spent hunting, harvesting our vegetable crops, and picking berries and boletes, followed by days of jarring, jamming, and storing away as much of the wild edibles as we could fit into our larder and whatever space remained in the freezers.

Winter was the season we lived for most though. Despite subsisting in a land where nights are so long the darkness lasts much of the day, we relished the intimacy that developed through months of traveling with our dog teams, more often from sunset to sunrise than the other way around (due to maintaining day jobs to support our dog habit). Whether in the slanted light of day, or under every phase of the moon and the enormous star-crowded skies of the evening, we journeyed hundreds—sometimes thousands of miles—each year with our canine companions, exploring the backcountry that makes up the bulk of Alaska.

Together, we stared out over snow-blanketed mountains, their blue-hued ridges fading lighter the further each fold of the landscape stretched to the horizon, then traveled the range from end to end. In the lowland valleys between them, we snaked along the serpentine curves of icy rivers and traversed seemingly endless expanses of frozen lakes and buried muskegs. Our faces, confettied in the cold, white currency of the season, hid the smiles beneath.

Whenever weary, we'd hunker down in the silent stillness and shelter provided within forests of dense spruce, basking for a few hours in the crackle and orange glow of a makeshift campfire before eventually curling up with the dogs, sleeping together for warmth and comfort.

Despite the perpetually inhospitable cold and the miles that separated us from more civilized society, in the hours and days of self-imposed isolation where we shared space only with each other and our dogs, we felt like we were in the best place we'd ever been or would be. In these far-flung locales where the only audible utterances of life were the soft panting of husky breath and the voices in our own heads, we were in our element. We felt happiness, experienced what it meant to us to be alive, and we found what we had come so far north searching for: our true selves.

This doesn't mean our lives as mushers were always bliss. All dog owners have their fair share of problems, and at times our struggles seemed compounded fortyfold. It's understandable that most folks tend to stay tight-lipped about the minor calamities and major catastrophes that constantly occur. Sure, tales are legion of all the things that can go wrong during the Iditarod, but few and far between are all the sordid stories that begin to accumulate from a life shared with forty dogs the other fifty-one weeks of the year.

Still, I believe it is the misfortunes of our dog-filled lives that define us, the misadventures we remember most vividly, and the mishaps that become the funniest stories to share with others. This book will divulge these embarrassing details, which at the time we wished had never happened but now are cherished and fondly retold for their humor, or significance, or for truths they reveal.

The driving force of sharing these stories is to give readers a glimpse of what it's like to truly live a half-feral Alaskan lifestyle as we have and still do, so they can vicariously experience and comprehend the magnitude of responsibility, and all the joy, pain, and myriad other emotions that come from the fabric of a life threaded through and through by the fur of forty dogs.

We don't own our dogs; they are a part of us, our lives inextricably intertwined. For those who spend more time around people than animals, this is a tough concept to comprehend. Looking at a yard full of high-strung huskies, most outsiders to our world don't see the individuals, distinctly dissimilar from each other. To most folks, they're merely different sized and colored canines. They don't see what we see. They don't understand the unique personalities or our shared histories with each one. But this is a chance to see it all.

This isn't just a rare opportunity to experience remote areas of Alaska without having to rough it, to know white-knuckle excitement without ever leaving the living room, and to briefly be part of the fraternity of the fur-clad without feeling the sting of Arctic air or ever fearing frostbite. More than that, these stories detail the dramatic communion between humans and canines, and in a way that is honest, authentic, and at times raw to the bone.

Through my words, I want people to see the puppy we caught at birth, seconds old, still wet and wriggling, but quickly growing within weeks to yip and yap to get us to play longer no matter how much frolicking we had already done. To witness the scared pup shivering in the corner of the sterile chain-link stall at the animal shelter, that prior to adoption was too afraid to even make eye contact with us, much less believe we could be the bearer of a new lease on life. To learn how awkward and gangly they all were once, tripping over their own paws the first time we harnessed them up and ran them in a team. To experience seeing the dogs that went on to excel at what we trained them to do and exceeded our expectations when their own primitive instincts and prowess for the outdoors took over.

With forty dogs comes forty deaths. You can't have the yin without the yang. In the following pages, readers will also come to understand you don't just pay heavy emotional dues; you take out a second mortgage on your heart. To feel the concern when the dogs' internal fires begin to burn down, their muzzles turn gray in retirement, and muscles that once bulged and rippled are replaced with a stiffness so painful we have to lift the dogs from their cushy beds and carry them outside to relieve themselves. To undergo the anguish and heartbreak that comes from standing by help-lessly as a companion you've known, and seen, and cared for everyday for a lifetime finally bears the breadth of elsewhere. To not only lose that friend, but have them die in your arms while you look into their eyes and unabashedly whisper in their ear how much they meant.

This book is an invitation to understand the essence of life with forty dogs in its entirety, and through that comprehension to truly appre-ciate what we see every day, and never take for granted how special it is. This is my goal, my purpose, my need—to share the intrinsic nature and indispensable quality that determines each dog and defines their unique character and personality. Not everyone can sacrifice their spare time, salaries, and sanity to get to know so many characters—from the well-mannered to the wily—but this book will reveal the endless adventures and misadventures that come to those, like us, who have made a life-changing canine commitment.

A Rogues' Gallery

N
O MORE STORIES AT THE POUND," COLE PLEADED, AS I WALKED in cradling the newest addition to the kennel, one of several in recent months to join our ranks after being abandoned or surrendered at the local animal shelter.

My wife's statement came partially in jest, since I always consulted her by phone beforehand, but like me, she found it difficult if not impossible to say "no" to a dog once we had actually experienced face-to-face contact. The animal's anonymity dissolved, no longer a static mugshot on a computer screen or newspaper ad with the words "For Adoption" over its picture. Peering into the eyes of a hopeful inmate at the pound—in fur and flesh—made them more real, made their plight more painful to ignore, made their prospect for living or dying an at-hand decision. In these moments, disregarding the opportunity to save a dog was inconceivable.

"We're running out of room," Cole said.

She wasn't wrong. At the time we didn't even own our home or property. We were living on half an acre of land, renting a cabin with the same interior square footage and charm of a small submarine. In that one-room residence existed all our worldly possessions: a frameless futon mattress that served as the bed; a folding card table with two metal chairs for eating dinner and hosting company; a twelve-inch television that

The pup we later named Ping stares longingly out of her cage at the Kenai Animal Shelter. We adopted her and her mother, whom we named Pong, the day after this picture was taken.

picked up (if you squinted) one channel; one pot, one pan, one teakettle, two sets of silverware, and a box with all our clothes.

In addition, we already allowed half a dozen dogs to live inside with us, including Ping and Pong—two others who originated from the pound a few weeks earlier. While working on a story about pet adoptions for the local newspaper, I spied the tiny pup we would later name Ping at the back of one of the sterile runs made of chain-link and concrete. Fuzzy, gray, and seemingly oblivious to the mere days she had left to live if not adopted, I felt my heart not so much melt as turn gooey with empathetic emotions. Her appearance also reminded me—almost exactly—of Goliath, a dog we had acquired a few months earlier, but whose cookie-sweet personality had won me over.

At the close of the workday I sped home to plead my case to Cole. She capitulated, but when I returned to the pound the next morning the tiny pup now snuggled with a full-grown but otherwise identical version of itself, which to my dismay I found out was its mother.

"Yesterday, we had them separated briefly for cleaning, but they came in together," said the shelter manager, a lanky, mustached man with a 1,000-yard stare I assume he developed from the same post-traumatic stress that causes it in soldiers—seeing too much death.

"They're not a package deal, but it'd be great if they went together," he added.

I stood dumbfounded, time pooling in the present as my mind worked through the decision it now had to make. I hadn't come for two dogs, nor did I desire to leave with two, but how could I live with myself if I only took home this pup, severed the bond between it and the only creature that unconditionally loved it till that point, and potentially doomed the mother to death by lethal injection should she hit the end of her allotted time span for adoption?

I knew I couldn't, and by the gleam in the shelter manager's eye, I think he knew it too. I called Cole to briefly explain these new circumstances.

"Well, saving the pup and killing the mom isn't my definition of a rescue," she said.

With that approval, not only did Ping come home, so did her mother, whom we named Pong.

Weeks later, when I returned to the pound for a follow-up story, I distinctly felt like a mark whose emotions the shelter manager knew could be played like a fish on the end of a line.

"Well, while you're here, take a look at this one. She may be a good fit for your program," he said, his arm on my shoulder, steering me to my future furry acquisition.

This time, the dog cowering at the back of the run seemed much more aware of the severity of its situation. I've seen circus elephants less sad than this pitiful pup. Its pelage was a traditional black-and-white Siberian husky pattern and mask, crisp and contrasting, but without the big-dog build. Instead, the pup had a more slender frame, slight stature, and a sleek rather than furry coat. Based on its small size and still-present milk teeth, it appeared around four months old.

"So, what's its backstory," I asked the shelter manager, trying to sound more indifferent than I felt.

"It's a female; came in overnight. We found her in the after-hours drop-off cages with five littermates, but the others were so feral and frightened, there was no way to put them up for adoption so I put them down," he said as casually as if asking how I take my coffee.

"There was a note, too. Left by a musher, that's why I thought it might be a good fit for you. Lemme see if I can find it," he said, and departed briefly. When he returned he handed me a wrinkled piece of loose leaf on which was scrawled the crude handwriting of either a near-illiterate person or a young child. The sparsely punctuated sentences read, "All of them are sled dogs very loving dogs need to be trained . . . very smart good sled dogs . . . please do not put down! Will be good for musher."

The plea moved me, deep to the marrow of my bones. Cole seemed equally entangled in emotion when I brought the dog home, because despite her vow that this should be the last pound pup, her sternness quickly melted away when I passed the newcomer over and the cute critter softly licked her chin. Cole didn't say anything, but as she ran her fingers through the pup's coat, I saw the intrinsic calmness that comes from petting a dog engross her. I knew we were in agreement that I had made the right decision.

"So what's this one's name?" she inquired after a few minutes.

"I was thinking 'Six,'" I said. It seemed appropriate for her, but also to somberly remember her five siblings who weren't so fortunate.

I think the reason saving Six was so important to me, and all the dogs that came afterward, stemmed from a childhood experience that was out of my hands. I was probably seven years old at the time, living with my mom and a stepdad, a real hard-ass, at least with me. Neither of them was ever really "doggy," but they made an attempt to meet my needs for having a canine companion by bringing home a mutt from the pound.

They picked it; I wasn't consulted at all, resulting in one of my first life lessons: beggars can't be choosers. But still, I marveled at the sight of this, my own dog. He was colored like an old penny, and bore all his proportions perfectly out of whack. He had an elongated torso and stubby little legs. His head was big, and his coat short. He looked like a cross between a Welsh corgi and an Irish setter or Labrador.

I fell in love immediately.

We called him Corky, although I can't remember if he came with that name or one of us picked it for him. Despite how friendly he acted with every member of the family, and how smitten I was with him, my parents had a firm no-dogs-in-the-house policy. Relegated to the back-yard, Corky became bored, and rightly so, since I still spent most of my days at school. He tunneled relentlessly, not only making the rear lawn an unsightly mess, which my parents weren't keen on, but when he dug all the way under the fence to freedom, he'd go on the lam for extended periods, something else which they frowned on.

After a few weeks or so they had a change of heart about keeping Corky. Just outside my bedroom door, they spoke in voices loud enough for me to hear about their decision, but when the step-douche came in, for some reason, even at that young age, I needed him to say it to my face.

"Could you hear our conversation?" he asked.

"No," I lied, knowing he knew I had.

"We've decided to take Corky back to the pound. You're just not showing enough responsibility," he said, blaming me, like the classic cliché of the bad carpenter who blames his tools. I showed as much responsibility as I had been taught, but—then and now—I don't think the decision had anything to do with me.

"Oh," I said, emotionally crushed, but refusing to give the man who hurt me then—and my mom thirty-five years later with his infidelities—even one tear. My first courage, perhaps.

He peered at me, expressionless, for a few seconds, then walked out without saying another word. The next morning Corky was gone from my life, but lingered in my memories, haunting me for years.

I felt guilt, initially questioning if I should or could have done more to keep him, but as I grew older, it was not knowing what had happened to Corky and the helplessness of it all that bothered me. In all likelihood, he was euthanized for failing in a second home; I hoped that wasn't the case, but had no way of finding out his fate for certain. I was a kid; they were the adults. They made all the decisions, including that one, because they lacked the commitment to honor the covenant of care between themselves and the canine they agreed to adopt. But as an adult, I swore to myself if I ever got another chance to save a dog, I would do my best to do better than they did.

. . .

OVER THE NEXT FEW YEARS—AFTER SCRIMPING ENOUGH TO PURCHASE our own parcel of raw land—we accumulated so many rescues, runts, and rejects from other kennels, it became a defining theme for our operation. As a result, we settled on "Rogues Gallery Kennel" for the formal appellation of the motley crew we acquired, all of which seemed to come to us through serendipity more than conscious selection.

Next came two males from Salcha, a rural mosquito-riddled area roughly forty miles south of Fairbanks. The story of them joining the kennel began after we received an urgent call for help from the neighbor of Martina Delp, a thirty-three-year-old fellow dog rescuer from those parts. Delp, a proudly independent woman who served in the Alaska Air National Guard, lived alone with the exception of her thirty-seven sled dogs—all rescues from the local animal shelters—along with horses, a cat, and an exotic lizard.

After she didn't show up for work one day, friends alerted authorities who checked on her welfare and were greeted with a grisly sight. They found Delp's lifeless body, and the cause of her death—as these responders pieced together from the scene of her repose—a tree she had been chainsawing clipped a power line as it fell. The live wire instantly electrocuted her.

Lynx and I enjoying a typical day in our life shared with forty dogs.
What kid wouldn't want to grow up like this?

Other than exchanging a few rescue related e-mails with Delp, we didn't know her at all, but we could ascertain—with absolute certainty—that thirty-seven dogs were a lot to find homes for quickly in even the best case situation, which this wasn't. Delp's family, who lived in the Lower 48 and Europe, were unable to accept responsibility for so many dogs. Also, Delp wasn't a professional racer, so her name didn't bring in the usual folks, eager to take home a dog as a connection to a famous person, glomming on to a bit of their limelight. Furthermore, these were dogs that had already been given up on once, considered damaged goods of a sort by most, so we knew from our own experiences that people would not be beating down the door to take them home.

Dogs aren't the only ones that run in packs, though. So, too, do dog rescuers. We linked up with a few others who homed huskies in our area and made the ten-hour drive north in a convoy of pickups carrying crates we knew would be filled with dogs on the return trip home.

We arrived near the end of the day. Despite it being late evening, it was mid-May, so the sun still hovered above the horizon, an orange ball giving off plenty of light and warmth. We cut to where the dogs were located in the backyard, ambling through a wild bouquet of blooming lupine coming into full violet-petaled pageantry. Not even a kiss of a breeze presented itself and the forest beyond the dog yard was briefly— until the dogs barking at our presence drowned out the sounds—alive with the whistles and warbles of chickadees. It would have been a pleasant day by Alaska standards, had we not been there to peruse the pets a dead woman left behind.

We found the experience painful but educational. We had never considered what would happen to our own dogs should we meet an untimely death. We assumed family members would come forward to take home what they could, but we had never made these plans formally, or even more important, legally. Fortunately for Delp's dogs, she showed foresight and filed a last will and testament detailing her wishes for her brood, but she had taken all knowledge of who was who to the grave with her. Her dogs' names, their ages and physical descriptions, and their medical histories were all unknown.

All the dogs looked healthy and well cared for, and they displayed the usual array of personalities. Some were overtly gregarious and completely overjoyed at meeting newcomers, wagging their tails so excitedly, they whipped themselves right off their own doghouses. Others were so timid that they refused any form of hand or eye contact and trembled in terror inside their house whenever we stepped near.

"Which ones should we take," Cole asked, over the drone of biting insects.

On the drive up we had agreed on two as the maximum we could financially afford to add to our kennel at that time. It seemed like so few, but a harsh reality of rescuing dogs and one that becomes a mantra for anyone who does it for any length of time is: you can't save them all.

"I think we should go for the ones least likely to find homes with anyone else," I said.

"Well, that rules out these guys," Cole said, gesturing with her hands in Vanna White–style over a pen of puppies roughhousing and chewing each other's ears in the elation of us standing so close.

We knew they'd be the first to go so we scanned the dog yard, staring past those literally jumping with joy, to essentially look for omega animals: any gimps, cripples, misfits, or weirdos. In the back corner of the kennel we found a likely prospect—an ancient, mole-dark male with a build as bizarre as a Salvador Dali painting. He had a head like a boar and a barrel chest to match, but his hips and stubby hind legs seemed half the size they should be.

"He looks like a weight lifter who does too much upper body, but totally neglects working out from the waist down," I joked.

"Looks more like the Tasmanian devil from the old Looney Tunes cartoons to me," Cole said.

The circle where he was tethered looked like a Word War I trench. There were long deep ruts where he clearly dug for many hours a day. There were a couple of huge, heavy equipment tires in his spot too, possibly to slow down his digging or divert him from the activity, but from the jagged rubber chunks all around the circumference, it was plain to see he chewed on them extensively. The filthy-looking animal also paced feverishly with his food bowl clamped in his jaws, staring more through us than at us. All of these behaviors added up to a dog with obsessive-compulsive tendencies. As if that weren't enough, we deduced after slapping mosquitoes next to his head without him taking notice, he was also completely deaf.

"I'd say he's a keeper," Cole quipped.

"Indeed," I concurred dryly, and with that, the dog joined our ranks and was from then on dubbed "Old Man."

"So who else?" Cole asked.

This time, our eyes searched past the messy mounds of freshly dug soil to a spot that barely looked like a dog lived there at all. Tall grass grew in the circle where he was tethered, indicating a cowardly creature that spent most of its time hiding in its house. The dog cowering at the back looked a lot like a coyote and exhibited a similar disposition: wanting to avoid human contact at all costs. Despite our best efforts to coax him out of his fear-induced catatonia, he wanted nothing to do with us. We were forced to manually, hand-over-hand, reel his chain in to bring him near. Like an anchor, he had to be dragged every inch of the way, his limbs locked up tight in resistance, as he was petrified stiff with fright.

"Looks like we found another addition," I said.

"At least he's younger than the other one," Cole said, since the dog appeared to be around two years old. This panic-stricken pup we named Rolo, due to his pale, caramel-colored coat. Our friends who drove up with us also took home seven dogs between the three of them. In the end, not all of Delp's dogs were able to find homes, but most of them did through the efforts of kindhearted people.

The nobility of these selfless deeds should not be understated. The bearers of bleeding hearts acknowledge it as both a blessing and a burden. Those who rescue dogs know an occupational hazard of compassion is that you eventually begin to deteriorate, deep within yourself, from seeing so much animal suffering firsthand.

Sure, there is joy and satisfaction from liberating a dog from an acutely awful situation, but those feelings are short-lived. Replaced by the dread of knowing there will be others, or worse still, the ones you can't save. There just isn't enough time, enough money, enough room, to save every dog in a bad way, which is why 2.7 million animals are euthanized in the United States annually. . . . I repeat, 2.7 *million* killed, *each and every year*, at the taxpayers' expense.

This number weighs on me, my conscience and my soul, till I feel like a dead man under six feet of soil. I dwell on this loss of dog life to the point I can't sleep at night, and when I do I have nightmares. My days are also filled with depression, which turns to cynicism and judgment, not just of those causing the suffering and their capacity to be so cruel and callous, but also of those who turn a blind eye to the hurt and dog deaths. If only people acted altruistically, if only those who aren't providing for dogs properly or adopting those without homes could be moved to act, if only more people would simply care. If only . . .

Then, just as my thought pattern of how humans could be so inhumane reaches near-obsessive proportions, others will come forward—

as with adopting Delp's dogs—and show they too care. Suddenly, there is *someone* else who understands sacrifices—like eating chips and salsa for dinner *for weeks* to afford premium-grade kibble—because they have also surrendered similar staples to provide for a dog in need.

It is then that I realize Cole and I are not the only ones who appreciate the underappreciated. We have kindred spirits—few and far between, but still out there—and knowing that these people exist, and are genuinely doing their parts to help animals, gives me the strength to go on saving lives.

. . .

NEXT TO JOIN OUR MOSAIC OF MUTTS WAS GHOST, ANOTHER FEMALE from our local animal shelter. She became permanent entirely by accident. I had been at the pound for a story when I spotted the gorgeous girl pacing in one of the runs. She had a short coat, white as the full moon, the only exception being her mauve-colored nose, the lightest of light blue eyes, and the black stencil that bordered them and her lips. Images of her exquisite appearance still echoed in my mind later that day when I visited our veterinarian with one of our other dogs, and I involuntarily described her during the appointment.

"I know someone who is looking to get a pet dog, and she sounds like a perfect fit for this person," he said.

Knowing time is of the essence when it comes to dogs on death row, and with the prospects of a home lined up, I shot back to the pound immediately. Getting there just before closing, I filled out the paperwork, forked over the adoption fee, and took the dog home. It was too late that day to make it back to the veterinary clinic before it closed, but I drove there the next day with the dog riding shotgun.

To my dismay, the veterinarian told me he had informed his friend of my find, but she had already made a doggy discovery of her own. It was premature of me to have adopted the dog, so I had no one to blame, just a new mouth to feed. We named her Ghost, partially due to her all-white color and partially due to the circumstances of her third-party adoption— that like an apparition—briefly manifested then disappeared.

Rowdy and all-white Ghost, another dog we adopted from the pound, lead a team around an ice-covered lake. Ghost excelled at leading the chase team.

Coolwhip followed a few weeks later, again from the shelter, but this time they called us. During past adoptions, I had mentioned in passing we already had a dog who suffered from an unusual medical condition, technically known as congenital laryngeal paralysis, informally known in Alaska as "wheezer" disease.

Pups with this inherited condition are born with a dysfunction in the nerves that control their larynx. Rather than moving normally, opening the airway during breathing, and closing to prevent choking on food and water, the throat muscles of a wheezer remain fixed in place.

In severe cases, nursing pups die when they are just days old, either from suffocation or by drowning from inhaling their mother's milk. In milder cases, pups survive and grow but have a raspy, wheezing sound to their breathing, and when playing or exercising will collapse in a gagging fit, their tongue and gums turning blue from lack of oxygen.

We had taken our other afflicted dog—Shagoo, given to us by another musher who couldn't afford to have her throat fixed—to the vet for the best corrective surgery that could be done at the time, at a cost of roughly $2,000 dollars. We couldn't afford it either, but paid the bill through the magic of maxing out credit cards. She came though the procedure breathing healthily enough to live life as a normal pet dog, but not quite capable enough to contend with the cardiovascular challenges of sled-dog training and competition.

"I figured since you had experience with this condition, you might be able to help this one too. Her owners brought her in after getting the wheezer diagnosis. They said there was no way they could afford to fix her," explained the shelter manager.

The dog he was referring to was an attractive young husky, a female, with a white coat splashed with numerous gray blotches and freckles on her muzzle, but based on her expression, she appeared to be suffering from mild mental retardation as much as impaired breathing. At all times a pink tongue dangled sideways from a big, open-mouth grin and her eyes, bright and blue as two robin eggs, were fixed wide open and goggled about. She seemed dumbstruck, as if having just seen the most amazing thing in her life, even when nothing out of the ordinary was happening.

"Why does she have a look like this is the greatest day of her life?" I asked.

"Maybe because it is," said the shelter manager, before walking away to leave me with what at this point was becoming an all too familiar decision-making process. He was clearly savvier than I first suspected. How had he missed an obvious calling to hawk used cars, I wondered.

Once home, I realized my initial psychological profile of the pup, which we named Coolwhip, was not that far off the mark. Inexplicably, she sometimes spent half an hour kangarooing in place on her hind legs and always with her tongue perpetually flapping in the breeze. Her hyperactivity, even as huskies go, exceeded normal levels. She embodied an exotic exuberance for life, like a zoo monkey that revels in throwing feces at spectators. She also belied the breezy being of a total free spirit, which is dog-owner-speak for a pup that lives by its own rules, not yours. Coolwhip listened selectively, responding to what she clearly perceived as verbal "suggestions" less than half the time, particularly when it came to being recalled when off leash.

When we brought her to the veterinarian for her initial post-adoption checkup, X-rays revealed in addition to her wheezer disorder, Coolwhip suffered from a separate condition known as megaesophagus, which is not as megacool as it sounds. Basically, the pipe used for gulping down food was oversized and too large to actually swallow food, even if her throat muscles worked properly, which they didn't. As a result, for the first six months of her life with us, we had to feed her while she stood upright, balancing on her hind legs, so gravity could transport the food downward to her stomach. Fortunately, as Coolwhip got older, she outgrew the engorged esophagus, but she remained a wheezer.

Being devoted to not just providing the best quality of life we can for our animals year-round, but also believing in doing what we can to contribute to the continually growing body of scientific knowledge about sled dogs, we volunteered Coolwhip for a study involving an experimental procedure. Not only would veterinarians—one flying in from Australia and the other from Germany—attempt to correct her wheezer condition, but taking part in the study allowed us to treat her at no cost.

Knowing Coolwhip was a wild child, for weeks before the surgery we kept her in the house in an effort to calm her down so she didn't hurt herself during her post-surgery recuperation. Everything had been going swimmingly until the night before her surgery, when the master of disaster made a mad dash.

Cole and I were in the kitchen making an evening meal when one of our house dogs, keen to paw the handle of the front door to let himself out, did so on this occasion. Without hesitation, Coolwhip launched herself off the couch, gleefully galloped out the entrance, and kept on going into the darkness of night as we ruefully looked on.

"Now what?" I asked rhetorically.

"We *have* to find her," said Cole. "The vets are only here *this* weekend. That's it. There's no way to reschedule."

I knew she was right, so begrudgingly and without dinner, we suited

We adopted from the pound Coolwhip, a hyperactive husky with a dismal diagnosis. With surgery, she overcame her condition, but this wild child's tongue flapping in the breeze was incurable.

up in our coats, boots, and headlamps and began what would be a bush-whacking search through the spruce stands that surrounded our home. Hours later, just past midnight, we gave up. We never got a hand on Cool-whip, but came tauntingly close a few times in what was for her surely a spectacular game of hide-and-seek. Hearing her loud, heavy breathing in the woods whenever she paused for air, we could zero in on her loca-tion, but by the time we thrashed through willow thickets and over downed deadfall, she would have caught her breath and tore out again. This happened dozens of times during the search; it was like playing a game of Olly-olly-oxen-free with an obscene caller.

The next morning we woke at 5:00 A.M. and after seeing no signs of Coolwhip we stuck to our original plan, which entailed running three teams of dogs before making the three-hour drive to Anchorage, since we knew the kennel would be shut down from training while we endured the city for a few days for post-operation monitoring of Coolwhip . . . should she return.

The deafening ruckus the dogs make during hookup can be heard miles away and is often enough to draw in even the most distant run-aways, and we hoped Coolwhip wouldn't be the exception. Our plan worked, but not when we needed it to. Just as we launched from the yard, with no way to stop the two twelve-dog freight trains for longer than a few seconds, Coolwhip sprouted from a thick copse of cottonwoods in front of the lead team.

Ecstatic at the idea of being chased once again, she took off down the opposite trail we were hoping to take, and our teams followed. This alternate route was too narrow for turning around and added another half hour to the run, which meant, even if we could miraculously get our hands on Coolwhip, we would surely be late to the surgery.

In a stroke of luck, Coowhip exhausted herself over the course of the training run, the result of intermittently leaping from the woods to briefly lope alongside us until out of oxygen, at which point she'd disappear back into the brush to suck wind till she caught her breath. When we rolled back into the yard, she stumbled in with us, and collapsed in utter exhaustion. Cole and I, almost in unison, set our brakes and then pounced on her.

Rather than relief, a wave of nausea overtook us. Coolwhip reeked from an all too familiar odor. Living next door to several commercial salmon fishermen, they will often—illegally and unethically—dump flounder, Irish lords, and any other by-catch that ends up in their nets, in a big pile at the outer edge of their property, right on the line between us and them.

Any loose dogs get chummed to the stench, to do what is perhaps the most mysterious of all their behavior: rolling around in the rotten pile and seemingly relishing the act of doing so. The funk Coolwhip came home with ranked somewhere between day-old road-kill and unwashed butthole. We knew it would constitute a sacrilege to operating-room sterility to arrive for a preplanned and majorly invasive surgical procedure with her coat so thoroughly contaminated.

We gave her not one, but two baths, extra heavy on the suds, and still there lingered a slightly noxious, breath-of-vulture-bouquet, but at this point we were so late for the procedure, there was nothing more we could attempt. We called the veterinarians, plead our sob story, and assured them we would be there as soon as we could.

As it turned out, other than the doctors' eyes watering up a bit from Coolwhip tainting the breathable air in the operating room, the surgery was a success. Coolwhip healed quickly over the next few weeks, and her breathing sounded almost indistinguishable from any other dog. Within months we were able to work her into harness and eventually she trained side by side with the best dogs in our kennel, and for many years afterward.

From a clumsy, breath-sputtering, inferior specimen, Coolwhip changed. It took a trained eye to see the subtleties of the strength embodied in her, much like how the average person can't detect how soft and flabby a caged lion looks compared to their wild counterparts who are more buff and bulging with muscles from chasing down dinner still on the hoof. Post-surgery, from the excessive exercise (that still never seemed like enough for Coolwhip), her physique developed a sculpted appearance, her chassis became chiseled, the muscles under her fur felt stony hard to the touch. Her whole demeanor evolved as well, once she realized running in harness with a pack was the perfect place to get her runner's high. She took to her position in the team with pleasure. We hadn't so much tamed her restless spirit as shifted it to our advantage.

As a pet parent, seeing Coolwhip's total transformation served as a testimonial for not giving up after even the most dismal diagnoses. The only analogy I can make would be seeing a small child afflicted with chronic asthma beat their condition and go from barely able to play sports to attaining a first-string position on the varsity team. It's more than joy, or pride, or satisfaction. It was a feeling of fulfillment for seeing something through to the end that in the beginning seemed so irreversible and impossible, but became realized, imaginable, and—hopefully to others with hopeless cases—inspirational.

. . .

FOR THE NEXT FEW MONTHS I AVOIDED THE ANIMAL SHELTER, knowing our passion for saving pets far exceeded our income, but heartless human acts aren't contained to one location. Two more dogs, brothers in fact, became incorporated with our doggy conglomeration after their original owner gave up on them and all the dogs in his kennel. He just walked away and abandoned them. I'd love to say this kind of thing isn't common in Alaska, but a sad reality is it happens every few years. Caring for a kennel requires a tremendous dedication of time, energy, and financial resources, and a lot of people leap into owning or breeding lots of dogs before they have thoroughly researched all the hard work the commitment will entail. Some quickly find themselves in over their heads, and will try to adopt out a few dogs. Others, of less conscience, will cull their numbers or bring them to the pound. And then those with no scruples will abandon their kennel, leaving the dogs to either starve to death or fend for themselves.

It was this latter type of human (and I use the word generously in this case) that brought the brothers into our lives. Several mushers with moral fiber better than his banded together to take in as many of the abandoned dogs as they could. Some had gone weeks without food and clean water and were in such a severe state of emaciation, euthanasia was deemed the most humane course of action. Other neglectees reverted back to a more feral state, and acted dangerously aggressive to those there to help. Several of these dogs were also put down.

Perhaps saddest of all, a litter of puppies had been born in the interim. Already a couple months old and with no human contact, they had developed hair-triggers. Scared out of their wits by two-legged intruders to their world, these whelps sprinted at such breakneck speeds they couldn't be caught by hand. Instead, landing nets, typically used for securing salmon, were required to capture the panic-stricken pups. Like the older dogs, some were deemed too feral to risk rehabilitating, but three little pups that curled into fetal balls from fear rather than attempting to snap and bite were granted the gift of their lives.

A rescuer who knew we had a track record of taking on huskies with tough or troubled backgrounds called, asking if we could take them. One pup, a coffee-colored female, was already spoken for by a young woman who assisted in the rescue, leaving two males. We agreed, sight unseen, to take them.

They arrived a few hours later, both with sunken brown eyes and thick matted coats as black and dirty as potting soil. The smaller one Cole named Boo—a nickname she called her little brother growing up. The other pup, slightly larger and with one floppy ear, I named Klaus—for no other reason than I liked the ring of the Germanic word.

After weeks of trust building, both came out of their shells, but entirely different personalities emerged. Boo exhibited affection and an eagerness to please. Off leash he tended to move in tandem with me, much like dogs that have gone through obedience class and stick to their owner's calf, step for step. He picked up fetch quickly and ran on such high octane that he could spend an hour sprinting without growing weary of it. Once he started training in harness with the rest of the kennel, he displayed a total lack of fatigue. His pure, gut-driven power quickly led to a permanent promotion running with the core race dogs.

Klaus also warmed into being very soft-hearted and friendly, but when off leash would spend a lot more time interacting with other dogs than us. He also enjoyed pulling a sled, but wasn't gifted with the same fitness and stamina as Boo. He never quit or ran with a slack line, but he fatigued earlier than the other dogs, struggled to keep up, and his body language at the end of a run epitomized a dog totally out of gas. We kept conditioning him for several years, but when it seemed he was just as happy spending time on the couch, we decided to retire him from running and gave him to Cole's mom and dad. He now spends his days in Massachusetts where he roughhouses with their other dog, a German shepherd, who like Klaus has a zero-tolerance policy for squirrels in their yard.

One of our greatest successes with a dog adopted from the local animal shelter became apparent when the gutsy gal made it the furthest, literally and figuratively. At this point, when working on a story at the pound, I dropped all pretenses of leaving without a dog.

"What've you got for me this time?" I asked the shelter manager upon arriving.

"Funny you should ask," he said with a sly smile, and led me to the back where a small female pup suspiciously eyed me at a safe distance from the front of the cage.

Wary and untrusting at first, my kissy noises and fingers waggling through the chain-link proved too much for her to resist. She leaned in broadside and let me scratch on her back. Her coat was thick and black with the exception of a white star on her chest, white toe tips, and a white wisp on her chin. Without protest I adopted her and unlike some pound spooks, this pup displayed an affectionate personality from the second she hopped in the cab of my pickup. She cuddled in my lap and nuzzled my beard the whole drive home.

This addition we named Arrow, like the dog in the Harry Nilsson song "Me and My Arrow." I also secretly hoped she would one day fly straight and true down the trail for us, and a few years later—after growing into a strong, but lean and lanky-legged runner—she did.

Cole signed up for the 1,000-mile Yukon Quest, known as the "Toughest Sled Dog Race in the World," an annual run between Whitehorse, Yukon Territory to Fairbanks, Alaska. It traverses some of the most pristine and last true wilderness areas in North America, following late 1800s Klondike gold rush routes and historic sled-dog-delivered mail trails. Teams must be self-reliant while navigating as much as 200-miles between some checkpoints, where challenges routinely include temperatures of forty below, savage winds smiting in excess of 100 miles per hour, soul-crushingly steep mountain ascents and descents, lonely and desolate labyrinths of winding frozen rivers and creeks, and all during a time of winter when nights are seventeen hours long.

Prior to this race, all the dogs had put in thousands of miles of rigorous training and conditioning, and Cole had won a few and done well in several 200- and 300-mile races around the state. However, all of these previous events had twelve-dog maximums, and the Quest allowed up to fourteen dogs. Cole knew starting with less than the required amount just meant more work for the other dogs on the team, so to have a full complement of fourteen she would need to take some unproven athletes. She decided on a yearling, Kawlijah, that had always been outstanding despite his young age, and Arrow, who had never raced before.

It was a tall task, but Arrow rose to the challenge. At every checkpoint, I'd be anxiously waiting, my bottom teeth raking my upper lip raw, fully expecting Cole to drop Arrow from fatigue, but each time she didn't I'd be pleasantly disappointed. To be honest, Arrow did appear bone-deep tired upon arrival, but after lapping up a hot wet meal, and getting a few hours' rest, she would leave with pep in her step.

In the end, Cole and the team finished twelfth out of twenty-nine teams that started the race, Arrow still there with her, still pulling, still contributing to the whole, and that was a truly noteworthy accomplishment. She had hauled a heavy load for 1,000 miles, something many dogs have tried, but not as many have succeeded at, and some that have succumbed to injury, illness, or exhaustion were dogs specifically bred for the task by some of the most recognizable names in the sport of mushing.

Sure, Arrow wasn't on a first-place team, but she wasn't on the last-place team either. Even if she had been, though, wouldn't it still have been an amazing feat? To put it in human terms, isn't the last person to cross the finish at the Boston Marathon or the Ironman World Championship triathlon still succeeding at an endeavor few people could achieve even if they dared try?

To me, it's not that pound dogs don't have worth, or to be more specific, inherent worth as sled dogs, it's just that to succeed with them you have to be open to finding their very individualized skill sets, and that's what we did with all of our rescues.

Pong, while she can't sustain sprint speeds for very long, can break trail at slightly slower speeds *for hours.* Ping's digestive processes move at a glacial pace, so much so that I think she could put on a few pounds from just a whiff of the food bucket, and this proved valuable when racing in deep-minus temperatures when dogs with higher metabolisms shiver off too much weight. Six, while small, can remember any trail after having only run it once, which I relied on whenever I grew disoriented or got lost from time to time. Rolo developed into an amazing gee-haw leader, turning left or right with precision whenever we gave the commands, which also helped all the dogs in line behind him learn the meaning of these words and the importance of listening to the musher. Ghost excelled at leading of a different sort, running at the front of a team chasing another, which is also useful for not burning out gee-haw leaders. Coolwhip's character trait of perpetually acting over-caffeinated made her invaluable as a cheerleader, where an always-barking dog late in a run can, and does, spread enthusiasm to the others. And Old Man, well, he was a bit too decrepit to ever contribute much to the team, but he always made me smile when I came out to feed the yard and saw him excitedly carrying around his food bowl, and that was enough to earn his keep.

There is elegance to seeing any dog team coalesce, and even more so when pound dogs are involved. People expect them to fail, or at the very least not succeed. Working through and watching them overcome this stigma is a reward far beyond bragging rights, prize money, or trophies for the mantle.

To me the process mirrors a mathematician working through a complex equation, sorting the fractions and getting the decimals in the right place, all the way to its end. It's not the simple things you stumble on, like fitting all dogs with the correct size harness and booties, although there are nuances to these tasks and satisfaction as well in learning who takes what piece of gear. The more exacting process is having the patience to learn their idiosyncrasies, to work through the socialization issues, to overcome their physical deficits, and figure out what role or which position in the team best suits them.

Basically, the formula for success requires—demands, really—truly getting to know the dogs on such a personal level that when you look at them, you begin to look past the flaws and see what their strengths are and create success with what you have, not what you wish you had. You don't see tools that are disposable; you see teammates that are indispensable and irreplaceable.

Because of all these intricate variables, there are a million ways for it to go wrong and only one way for it to go really right. But when it does, when you begin to feel mastery where once only mayhem existed, and everything finally fits into its proper place, it's like Einstein's theory of relativity. It all works and makes sense. And if there is one main difference between sorting out a math computation from a mushing conundrum, it's that with the latter the sum ends up being far greater than the whole of its parts. Numbers merely change, but dogs transform—from hurt, to healed, to heroic.

Doubter and Goliath

INITIALLY BUILDING OUR KENNEL FROM ROGUES, RUNTS, AND rejects from other mushers and the pound, we were getting pretty used to the petty comments and second-guessing of skeptics regarding our ethos of running the motley crew of dogs we had gathered to the best of our—and their—ability. Never, though, had someone so directly nay-said one of our beloved brood as just before Cole won the Gin Gin 200 Sled Dog Race.

The dig came the night before the competition. Cole already had a lot on her mind, knowing the next day she would be vying for victory against some of the biggest names in dog driving, several with egos even bigger than their race résumés. We had driven all day and into the night, and booked our accommodations at the banally named Paxson Inn, along with nearly the entire race field. While the somewhat shabby hotel could be critiqued on many things, its reputation for welcoming dog mushers was beyond reproach.

A cavalcade of dog trucks pulled in all evening, parking one beside another, and left idling for many hours to keep the murmuring engines warm and working in the minus thirty temperatures. These trucks would eventually be turned off late in the night, and then plugged in—using special cold-weather heating features—to keep the battery and oil in the pan at least lukewarm. In the meantime, the extended tailpipes—running vertically up the back of the truck to vent above the boxed dogs' breathing areas—belched clouds of thick fumes into the cold night air.

We had all the dogs tethered to the truck by way of drop chains, long lengths of which ran along each side of the vehicle and attached at anchors on the front and rear bumpers. The dogs get clipped to individual, roughly one-foot lengths, that extend from these main lines. The dogs stay in the locked dog boxes during transport and to sleep at night, but are let out and put on the drop chain during the breaks on the commute to stretch, eat, and relieve themselves. This system keeps them safe on road trips.

Our dogs were all tethered and eagerly lapping at their dinners, brimming bowls of blood-soaked kibble and ground beef, liver, and tripe. Another musher, famous for his own winning race record as well as being a bit arrogant, parked next to us and while feeding his own hungry huskies, he glanced over.

"Don't tell me this is one of your racing dogs," he condescended, while looking down his nose at Goliath. "There's no way—no way—this dog could be good. Look at that coat!"

We were aghast at the statement. As Leonhard Seppala (a legendary musher who played a pivotal role in the life-saving 1925 serum run to Nome) once said, "In Alaska, our dogs mean considerably more to us than those 'Outside' can appreciate and a slight to them is a serious matter."

In mushing, if not all sports, there prevails an attitude that until you're a somebody, you're a nobody, so having this stranger act overtly rude to our faces was nothing new. What irked us more was his disbelief in Goliath—based on a mere glimpse. The piercing comment questioned the character of a dog that had for years dutifully served as one of the pillars of our race team, and whose unwavering endurance often made the difference between our success or failure.

To be fair, Goliath's humble appearance and shy demeanor can be a bit misleading, and over the years many had read his introversion as synonymous with athletic impotence. Even Goliath's original owner had cast doubt on him from the start, deciding to give his whole litter away while they were still tiny youngsters.

"I wouldn't expect much from 'em, I had an accidental breeding on Iditarod and neither the female, or male that bred her, was that impressive," the musher said, as we looked into a makeshift pen where several small pups were enthusiastically gnawing on the rib cage of a moose carcass from the inside out. They looked like a bunch of prisoners trying to chew through the fleshy-red and bony-white bars of their cell. Not expecting this litter to mature into up-and-coming champions, it appeared the pups were being fed modestly, making due on scraps such as the ruminant's remains.

We feared for the future of these unplanned pups in an already overcrowded dog yard, especially since Cole and I were just starting to build a race team back then. To us the idea of getting a pup from dogs that made the cut for an Iditarod team seemed like better odds than what we were getting at the pound, where the sire or dame of some of our dogs—based on their adult appearance—had genetics ranging from greyhounds to malamutes, and several breeds between.

"We'll take them," we said.

As it turned out, the musher had already promised several of the dogs to other people, so we ended up with only one: a small, smoke-gray little fuzz ball with eyes as sweet and brown as root beer.

Despite his ignoble inception, we had high hopes for the dog he would grow to become. In those early years, until we learned to look for each dog's individual strength and then utilize it, we longed for the type of hard-charging husky superstar we perceived existed in every successful kennel. In Goliath's case, when he came into our lives, I was reading a book by Jane Goodall and in those pages lived a chimp named Goliath who, while small, was extremely brave. Hoping our new addition might one day display a similarly noble personality characteristic as this ape, we dubbed the dog with the same name.

We fell in love with Goliath immediately, but some of our other dogs took convincing. Shagoo, one of our cantankerous house dogs, greeted him in her usual manner: by promptly biting him in the muzzle, opening a huge gash. The wound eventually healed, leaving a scar he still has to this day, and like many traumatic events, the memories lasted longer than the injury. For months afterward Goliath gave Shagoo a wide berth, and fearfully whimpered and whined whenever she menaced him with her sinister appearance. In order to stay safe from the canine equivalent of Hannibal Lecter that he lived with, Goliath spot-welded himself to me, and an inseparable bond became forged.

At first it was about protection for Goliath, and he sat in our lap for safety, but over time his presence became commonplace regardless of where Shagoo lurked. During the workday, he rode shotgun with me when I went to the office, and sat in the driver's seat people-watching for hours on end. Unlike some puppies who would thrash the inside of a vehicle if left alone, Goliath didn't mind the solitude, and would only cause damage if Cole or I forgot a morsel of food somewhere in the cab. He demolished a bag of Doritos once in the few moments I stepped away to pump gas. All that remained from his nacho-flavored lapse in judgment were tiny crumbs showered across the driver's seat and telltale neon-orange whiskers on his muzzle. Another time I tried to ward him off from woofing down my lunch by putting a six-inch sandwich in the center console, but like a termite dining on dry pine, he chewed his way through the interior upholstery, boring a big enough hole to get at my pastrami.

In the evening, when we turned our attention to conditioning our dogs, we were able to channel Goliath's energy in a more positive direction. As with the workday, it was too risky to leave him home alone with Shagoo, but Goliath was too young to be put in harness, so we let him free-run alongside the adults. By four months old he would pace the team for twenty miles, smiling the whole way, his pink tongue flat and dangling from the side of his mouth. By six months old he seemed to understand the older dogs were connected to the gangline, so he started to actually try to insert himself into the team by squeezing between two dogs, pacing them.

Goliath developed into a strong and sturdily built dog, similar in appearance to a small timber wolf. He never weighed in at more than fifty pounds, but had a boxy muzzle, deep chest, muscular haunches, and a luxuriously thick coat even for a husky, complete with sable-coloring and a plume tail.

Goliath is an Iditarod and Yukon Quest veteran, but despite his racing resolve, he relishes curling up on the couch, especially when he can cuddle with the family.

When not running, his favorite pastime is to share couch space with me or Cole, and there he exudes contentment. Reclining lengthwise on a love seat in the living room, it has become an evening ritual for Goliath to warmly drape across one of us like some kind of comfortable quilt. All is right in the world for him as long as I run my fingers through his lush fur, and to be honest, when his comma-shaped nostrils flare and his soft cheeks puff with each snoring exhale, all is right in the world for me too.

More than any other member of the kennel, for the first year of his life Goliath spent almost the entirety of his days with us, and slept through the night at the foot of the mattress on the ground we called our bed. As he grew old enough to officially train by pulling in harness, it became clear—perhaps from being inseparable for months—that Goliath's devotion to us was absolute. He displayed a strong sense of loyalty and an unwavering need to please.

Being one of the thickest-coated dogs in our kennel, he did struggle several times—mostly on hot days—as any marathon runner likely would if forced to exercise in a heavy parka. But Goliath never let himself fall behind the other dogs, never lost his will to continue pulling. He kept his tug line as tight as any of the other shorter-coated dogs.

The same held true as the runs got longer and more arduous, and he began to make the cut for several 200- to 300-mile races. He developed a self-assuredness about him, particularly when in lead. His niche seemed to be out front, exploring new trail, listening for commands to gee or haw. This confidence in him built incrementally with each run, and over the years it began to bleed into other areas of his personality, the culmination of which came when he finally cultivated enough courage to stand up to his lifelong bully.

It happened while Goliath intoxicatingly gnawed on a long femur bone from a moose, a treat we had given him after a hard day of running. Shagoo swaggered up and stared Goliath down expecting him to flee in fear as he always had done, but instead he locked eyes with her, curled a lip to bare his sharp white teeth, and emitted a guttural growl that even made the hair on my neck stand up. Shagoo read the message loud and clear: Goliath was no longer a little pup she could pick on, and they both knew it, from that day on.

Like his courage, Goliath's endurance also became nearly inexhaustible as the years passed and he grew into the prime of his athletic life. Even in those rare instances when we could read fatigue beginning to build in him, he never slowed down or gave up until the job was done. He always found that last gear and rallied to the finish line. Sure, there were a handful of times he had to be picked up late in a race because he was too tired to continue, but *we* made the decision in his best interests. He *never* quit on us.

Goliath's willingness to perform was tough to spot to the casual observer though. At hookup, a time when the excitement level of most dogs reaches critical mass, Goliath seemed to keep his excitement in check, internalizing his emotions.

While the dog next to him would be shrieking in frenzied excitement, springing vertically into the air with cappuccino-thick foam bubbling from its mouth, Goliath would grab a mouthful of gangline and quietly tug on it in eager, albeit subdued, anticipation while simultaneously leaning as far away from his running partner as his lines would allow. He felt as jazzed as any other dog in the team, he just showed it differently. He had vigor and skill, and his own distinct style, all of which could be said about most of our dogs. But Goliath had more than that even, a trait the others didn't. He had couth.

All of this is what made the loudmouthed musher's disparaging comments a jab in my side, and Cole's too, but we fought back our initial urge to bludgeon him with the feeding ladle in our hands and kept our cool. We casually looked over at this guy's own dogs, made up mostly of German short-haired pointer crosses: hybrids known to be fast, but with the trade-off of thinner coats and less body fat, two things that can really keep a dog warm.

Much like linear algebra and interpretive dance, this is something I've never understood. Why when racing in some of the most inhospitable weather on the planet—where the mercury routinely plummets to hellish depths where the burn is a cold one—would anyone intentionally breed for speed at the cost of a thick, potentially life-saving, coat of fur?

"Yeah, his coat is a bit thicker than what your dogs have got, but he's a finisher in these kinds of cold conditions. You'll see tomorrow," I said, trying to make it sound more like a compliment to Goliath than a challenge to this musher.

"We'll see," he said without the slightest note of interest, then snickered in a patronizing manner and went back to minding his own business, not a moment too soon for us.

The next morning we were greeted with a race report that seemed quite pleasant in terms of our experiences with this event in the past. The trail was said to be hard-packed and fast, the winds calm, and the daytime temperature predicted to be a comfortable minus twenty for the start, with a dip to minus forty-five at night for the portion of trail that ran along the frozen Susitna River where the denser, colder air always settled.

This prerace narrative promised a much better situation than Cole and the dogs faced in the past. She had competed in three of the previous four years, including the brutal 2008 race, when the weather was nothing short of a maelstrom. Hurricane-force winds combined with savage cold to make a windchill of minus eighty-five. It was a race where Cole really cut her teeth as a musher.

From the beginning of that race, the wind moaned in an eerie, unearthly manner. Foreboding snow dunes had been carved and their wild, sinuous shapes erased all signs of the packed trail along with the lathes marking the way. Some mushers became disoriented or disheartened and turned around before the halfway point. A few had to be rescued by Army National Guardsmen who happened to be volunteering for the race to practice their own cold-weather training skills.

Other teams were literally picked up by the wind and blown down into an easily fifty-yard-deep couloir with other racers that had suffered a similar fate. There, past the precipice, huge tangles occurred that required the dangerous task of taking hands out of mittens to unclip and re-clip dogs into the ganglines in order to straighten them out. In those temperatures, flesh becomes frostbitten in a matter of seconds.

Many of those who were skilled—or just plain lucky enough—to eventually make it to the finish, didn't do so unscathed. Some had minor frostbite to their faces or fingers, and at least one musher with improper boots cold-burned both his big toes black as coal, and eventually had to have them amputated to prevent gangrene.

We were shocked and saddened to see how many veteran mushers, including past Iditarod champions, were caught ill-prepared and hadn't packed proper cold-weather protective gear for their dogs—garments such as fleece or windproof jackets, and most importantly for the males, fox-fur jockstraps, informally called "peter-heaters." As a result, numerous huskies in other teams hit the finish with frostbite to their ears, tails, and most painfully of all, their penis-sheaths and tips.

Cole, on the other hand, went into every race hoping for the best, but expecting the worst. She had planned and packed for the frozen hell she had encountered and as a result, her team looked as good at the finish line as they did 200 miles earlier at the start. I wasn't the only one who noticed: so did the race marshals, who presented Cole with the Humanitarian

Award, a coveted prize given to the musher who displays the best dog care during the event. This was in addition to her second-place prize money.

It was the third time she had placed second in the race and Goliath was on her team for each event, but for this running—even before the other musher had shot off his mouth—Cole wanted to whittle her placement in the standings by one more spot.

We scrutinized over past years' training-mileage journals looking for areas to make improvements. We swam the dogs in a nearby pond for cardiovascular conditioning during the warm weather months, and from the time the Alaskan winter began to kill summer in its inimitable way—by smothering the world in that intermediate color that has no color—Cole and I rigorously trained the dogs by having them pull us on four-wheelers. For weeks we endured gray rain falling from gray clouds in a completely gray sky, as we conditioned teams on beaches with gray sand, gray stones, and next to gray water. Our world was gray, but we sucked it up in the hopes of having the dogs peak for this Gin Gin, and peak they did.

The first fifty-mile leg went great for Cole. She had the fastest time of the whole race field and couldn't believe it. I too competed in the race with a puppy team, and by the time I came in to the first checkpoint, she had been there long enough to have finished all her chores. I was kneeling down, rubbing balm onto the wrists of one of my dogs when she found me.

"I'm leading and don't know how. I'm the most conservative musher I know and I'm rating them down on the down hills," she said in a giddy sense of disbelief with her own performance.

"That's great, hon," I said sincerely from under the heavy weight of my fur-lined parka hood. "But shouldn't you be asleep by now?"

"Can't," she replied. "Too excited."

I did my best to get her to go lie down for at least a little while. She never did get in the winks she should have, but it didn't seem to hold her back. I came out of the lodge that served as a checkpoint to see her and the team off. In the distance, even in the low light I could see Goliath leading the charge out. His coat looked silver in the pale blue light of the quarter moon.

On the second leg of the race, the course followed the always frigid 110-mile run down the river. It was a long, long night run and with the mercury plummeting to the predicted minus forties or below for most of the trip, it made for an inhospitable evening.

For those who have never experienced these temps, or exposure to them beyond walking to and from the car on a cold winter morning, they are tough to endure for any length of time, but spending fourteen hours in them while standing still and fatigued on a sled is *absolutely* brutal.

Take this as a powerful statement coming from a musher, since being warm is as a temporary condition in the existence of any musher worth their salt, but minus forty and below is beyond cold. Soft winter clothes suddenly make sounds like crinkling vinyl. Every breath you take stings your teeth and sears the whole way down your throat and into your lungs. Eyes must be blinked frequently and any wind—no matter how slight—will make them water with tears that freeze almost instantly. Touching the brass snap of a dog's neck or tug line without a glove will leave a blistering second-degree burn. Even your bones seem to feel brittle and frozen.

Still, not even a cold comparable to when the mastodons ruled this region could get Cole down. Part of it is her perpetually positive disposition. Deep down she has always had a soul as warm as a summer's day that she draws energy from seemingly without trying or even knowing she is doing it. But on this night, a spectacular show going on overhead, and the dancing astral light of a rich, emerald aurora kept Cole from focusing on her numb fingers, toes, and nose. She maintained her race lead with thick-coated Goliath—seemingly at ease running in these temperatures—comfortably being her front dog much of the way.

On the third leg of the race, the last hilly forty miles to the finish, Cole continued to stretch her lead and again had the fastest run time of any of the racers. In the wee hours of the morning, to the fanfare of only a dozen or so people still up at that time, she came into the finish line with the team still raring to go. All the dogs were covered in a thick hoar frost that had built up from running through the steam cloud of their own exhalations. Back at the truck, after the dogs had their harnesses slipped off, received a light massage from Cole, and had all inhaled a warm, wet meal of meat and kibble, some still had the energy to wrestle and play.

Goliath, even though he's grown too old to seriously train with the team, still loves to run along with the other dogs, and frequently assumes the lead position.

A clever reader may be asking themselves, how I would know, since I was still on the trail when Cole came in. I know because it was relayed to me and the rest of the race field during the finishing banquet when Cole was awarded with her first-place trophy and prize money, and bestowed with the Humanitarian Award again.

"Anyone who saw her team at the finish line would know why she was chosen for this award," said the race marshal, and then continued to extol the ways Cole embodied the best example of the bond between dog and man, or woman in this case.

Winning the Humanitarian Award is always a prestigious honor whenever received, but circumstances in which this distinct privilege goes to the race winner are extremely rare. Sometimes to achieve victory, mushers will run their dogs hard, *really hard*, some could argue a little too hard, so the winning team frequently doesn't look and feel as good as they should and the race judges pick up on that.

For Cole's win, she didn't drive the dogs to extremes, or even outside their comfort zones to stay in front of the competition. Rather, she had a clean run, her training was specifically dialed in for this event, and that resulted in the team peaking as desired. Basically it lined up exactly as planned. So, to get the Humanitarian Award too, it really spoke to *how well* Cole cared for the dogs, before and during the race, and since we're always trying to foster the message of excellent dog care, it was gratifying to come out on top *and* be recognized for this devotion. The icing on the cake though came the next day as we grabbed a final bite to eat before getting on the road to head home.

This wasn't Cole's first win and we were familiar with the experience of Cole being treated differently after she came in first. Like high school, everyone suddenly wants to sit at the cool table. Mushers who a day before wouldn't give you the time of day are now eager to come introduce themselves and pull up a chair to eat with you, or perhaps buy you a beer. To our surprise, the prerace nay-sayer—who ended up finishing a few spots behind Cole—sought us both out, and instead of currying our favor over a greasy cheeseburger or bottle of booze, he made a sincere apology.

"Ya know, I gave you a bit of a hard time about that dog with the thick coat, but he made the whole thing, and I'm not too proud to admit I was wrong," he said. Then, turning specifically to Cole he humbly concluded, "Impressive run, Colleen. I'll never doubt your dogs again."

"For the record, he finished in lead," Cole replied, to punctuate Goliath's performance.

It meant a lot to both of us that this musher was man enough to come and admit his error, but particularly that the added accolade came from a racer as accomplished as we knew this man to be. Our team, Cole's performance, and Goliath's contributions in particular had left a lasting impression with this seasoned race veteran. We've always believed in our dogs unequivocally and unconditionally. In that memorable moment, despite how brief it lasted or fleeting it might have been for this other musher, it was nice to know someone else saw our dogs the way we always do.

Horsing Around

R EALIZING I WAS NO LONGER ALONE, I DROPPED THE AX AND rubbed my bloody palms on the pant legs of my insulated work bibs. I hadn't noticed the visitors at first, and now was feeling a little self-conscious about standing at the center of a thick coagulated puddle, and so many scarlet splatters beyond that, making the once-white snow around me look like a homicide scene.

I had woken up early, before the weak winter sun had risen, to begin cutting on the carcass while Cole went to work. Having already skinned it, and carved most of the meat off the bone in huge chunks, I was in the process of using my ax to chop out a rack of ribs when the vehicle pulled up my particularly long, purposefully secluded driveway. In that moment I had to have looked like a murderous lumberjack enthusiastically re-creating the infamous door-hacking scene from *The Shining*.

It didn't help that I had barely slowed my swing when they first arrived. I had the radio blasting, so didn't hear their vehicle's engine, but uninvited guests always induce a hullabaloo from the dog yard. The explosion of barks announcing their arrival is what caused me to stop my now public display of dismemberment.

Leaning on my ax while I caught my breath and feeling my pulse come down from near–heart attack levels, I could see several well-dressed women and a male teen all nervously talking amongst themselves in a magenta minivan. Finally, after a few minutes, the boy must have drawn the shortest straw because he exited the vehicle and approached with clear apprehension.

Dressed in a dark suit, starched white shirt, and black tie, he walked to within a few yards of me and my carnage and then opened with, "Can I ask what you're doing?" It was obvious, from his wide eyes and the porcelain hue of his face, he was sincerely asking.

"I'm cutting up some meat for them," I explained, waving my arm toward the dog yard. "It's . . . or rather, it *was*, a horse."

He nodded thoughtfully, processing the information for a minute, but must have deduce nothing too nefarious was taking place. His safety secured, he didn't waste any further time and cut to the chase.

"Do you have a few minutes to talk about Jesus Christ?" he asked.

I thought about it and said, "Sure, if you don't mind helping me finish this."

MUSHERS ARE MANY THINGS: RESOURCEFUL, THRIFTY, MISERLY, CHEAP. Whatever term you want to use, mushers tend to get good at saving a buck because the expense of running even a small kennel necessitates counting every penny. Dog food is exorbitant. And we're not feeding the run-of-the-mill grocery store chow, but a specially formulated kibble with higher percentages of protein and fat to aid the dogs' abilities to build muscles and contend with keeping on weight while burning thousands of calories per day from running.

In order to offset the food bill, we've had to get creative over the years. We stop by the local food bank weekly for any meats aged past "human grade," and in summer we hit up canneries and local fishermen to collect salmon heads, which are cast off as waste but actually packed with nutrients for the dogs.

However, of all the free dog food we get, nothing could compare to the mother lode of meat that results from getting a call to harvest a dead horse. These calls can translate into thousands of dollars saved and an equal weight in pounds of red meat once butchered, not to mention all the organs—such as the liver and heart—they relish like a delicacy.

Almost nothing is wasted. We'll run a hose through the stomach and intestines before offering the dogs a savory meal of tripe. We'll also give them all the long, white leg and rib bones, from which the dogs first tear off the little strips of still-dangling sinew, and before long, they'll gnaw down into the deep marrow. They even get the round, black hooves to chew on for enjoyment. Really, the only parts of the animal that will go unused are the lungs, hide, mane, and tail.

Since our dogs that normally eat—in addition to other supplemental meat products—a forty-pound bag of food a day (at a cost of $36 a bag at the cheapest), each horse will amount to a savings equivalent to about twenty-five bags of food (around $900).

Having horse meat also comes in handy once the racing season begins. Out on the Iditarod and Yukon Quest, they can get pretty worn down from running for 1,000 miles. Like us when full-body fatigue sets in, sometimes they'd rather sleep when they stop instead of eat. Other times, they may come into a checkpoint hungry, but become disinterested in eating the same snacks at each layover. Whereas having something novel like horse really excites the dogs and whets their appetites.

This smorgasbord may seem a bit macabre, but true Alaskans are a pragmatic bunch who believe just because an item or individual is gone doesn't mean something useful can't come from what is left behind. Perhaps it's from living in a place with such long winters, where everything must be stretched to last and in the old days not having enough meant not always making it. Or, possibly, it's that many who come here remember from the city lives they've left behind all the problems that can come from wanton waste. It's tough to say for certain, but in my experience, most horse owners would rather know their dead equine went somewhere besides the cold ground and became something other than worm food.

It's also not always about ecological efficiency. Sometimes it's about practicality or staying safe. In winter, the ground freezes deep, and as hard and solid as a bank vault's door, so any horse owner who hasn't already excavated a hole for their recently departed equine isn't likely to be able to do so until spring or even summer. And, as the days get warm enough to finally dig, so too do the bears come out of hibernation, ravenous for any source of protein, which easily includes the decaying carrion of a long-dead horse.

A neighbor of mine had a horse die in his backyard one spring and acted a bit lackadaisical in regard to doing anything about it. As a disclaimer, he was a guy who flourished in a neighborhood without a homeowners' association. To focus on just the largest items, no less than a dozen rusted trucks sat on his lawn (if waist-high grass constitutes a lawn) all in the state of disassembly they were left in after officially declared "broken down." So the horse initially didn't stand out among the overwhelming assortment of junk in varying forms strewn about.

That is until a behemoth of a brown bear boar took up residence right on top of the long-stiff stallion. The bruin ate what he could, then fell asleep across ribs as large as barrel staves, to defend the dead horse from any would-be scavengers, including the humans who lived there and now urgently wanted to remove the carcass. Their attempts were met with bluff charges, popping jaws, and the intimidating swat of a paw with five-inch-long claws—large enough to take a man's head off. The Alaska Department of Fish and Game finally had to be contacted to resolve the issue.

OUR FIRST CALL FOR A HORSE CAME FROM A COUPLE LOOKING TO AVOID such a scenario. They were young, twentysomethings, down from the city to house-sit for the parents of one of them—a reed-thin girl with flaxen hair who we soon found out was by far the more masculine of the two, at least in terms of dealing with deceased barnyard animals.

"We didn't know what to do with it, so I called my parents and they said call a musher," the girl explained from the other end of the line.

I was at work at the local newspaper when I got the call, but have always found showing up presentable for an office job a taxing endeavor. I long ago resigned myself to stretching my Casual Friday wardrobe over the five-day workweek, and as such was dressed suitably enough to go straight to the horse. Cole was dressed the same for similar reasons, but wearing her favorite forest-green "Kenai Peninsula 4-H" sweatshirt, so we left work early and headed to Sterling, a rural area where a lot of farmers and livestock owners live.

It was sweltering by Alaskan standards as we pulled into the paddock. The summer days were long, and the sun beat down mercilessly on the chestnut-colored quarter horse now in permanent repose. Hundreds of plump-bodied flies had already gathered and we knew it wouldn't be long until this horse was giving off a stink capable of chumming in bears for miles around.

One look at the young couple and we knew this situation was the deep end of a pond they never learned how to swim in. Not wanting to get dirty they had worn rubber hip waders, typically used for fishing in waist-deep water. Shaking hands with the young man further escalated my fears about how much work we'd get out of them. Not just limped pawed, but also the skin of his palm felt as soft as a puppy's belly rather than tough and calloused. The girl's hands were covered by ruby-red rubber dish-washing gloves, so I couldn't initially gauge her grit.

Even more unfortunate for us, the horse died in a part of the pasture cluttered with trees. These obstacles prevented us from backing right up to the animal, and the house sitters lacked the approval—and I suspect know-how—to use any heavy equipment to help us lift the quickly bloating beast into the bed of my truck.

"Any chance we could butcher, or at least gut and quarter the animal right here, so we could load it in manageable pieces?" I asked. I had packed my knife set for just such an eventuality, but all color flushing from their faces told me the answer was "no" even before the words "we'd rather you didn't" left the girl's lips. So we had but one option: doing it the old-fashioned way with a lot of heavy lifting.

We backed as close as we could and from the tailgate I put out boards to use as a makeshift ramp. With the hand-crank winch I also brought and attached to tie-off eyelets in the truck bed, the plan was to drag the horse up. We got everything in place, but when we started to winch the animal —now starting to loudly flagellate from the gasses building up internally— it weighed more than the maximum load the eyelets could bear. They popped off like pellets from a scattergun, rendering the winch useless.

This complicated everything.

We made a few feeble attempts to winch it from nearby trees, but the device was a puny, poor man's special (like I said mushers are pretty frugal) and not made for hauling the dead weight of a 1,200-pound horse, even if we could have gotten the correct angle, which we couldn't.

We knew we needed a new plan, so after a lot of head scratching and a little bit of swearing, we rolled the horse onto a tarp, then wrapped it around the beast like a burrito. Two of us pulled from the bed: Cole on the long black mane and me on the tail. The young couple stayed on the ground pushing, and using two-by-fours like leavers, but we kept losing our purchase on the horse as its corpse shimmied up the ramp.

We needed a fifth person, so I called an acquaintance from work, a recent transplant from Vermont. He promptly showed up in wingtip loafers, pleated khakis, and a baby-blue oxford button-down with the sleeves rolled to his elbows.

Clearly he was ready to work.

The only way it could have been worse was if he'd shown up with a monogrammed handkerchief in his breast pocket, but at least he showed up. A lot of lesser men would have declined my offer once the details were revealed.

Through the horde of flies, we commenced to pushing and pulling, grunting and straining, a little more swearing, and lots of sweating throughout it all. The couple looked like city slickers, but they worked like farmhands. After a few hours—amazingly without any pulled muscles or broken bones—we finally managed to get the hoofed heavyweight into the bed, mostly anyway.

Its stiff legs extended straight toward the sky, and once we closed the tailgate the horse's head was a little too large to fit all the way in due to the onset of rigor mortis, so we had to drape it over the tailgate. With nostril flaps drooping, pale tongue dangling, and eyes clouded with the opaque haze of death, I won't deny it was a ghastly scene, but we had no other way to transport it home.

Instead I focused on the positive. We had managed to move a mountain of dead weight and because of that I felt like I had conquered

Denali. My arms were limp and rubbery from fatigue, the muscles in my back sore and tight, and I was soaked to my socks with sweat, but happy to have the bulk of the heavy lifting behind us. Cole and I still had to go home and butcher it for several more hours, but the couple's problem was getting ready to pull out of the pasture.

With everyone feeling pretty pleased with our group performance, I had my buddy snap a quick photo of us with the horse, so we could remember the herculean feat of strength and Edison-like ingenuity we'd all just displayed to accomplish a mutual goal. Also, at the time I maintained an active blog about our year-round mushing lifestyle, primarily for our families and friends in the Lower 48. I thought the image would encapsulate a day in our life.

I was a little embarrassed because at that time, I had lost a competition at my work to see who could grow the longest beard before either the itching became unbearable or the publisher physically throttled one of us for not being office-presentable. The contest rules stipulated whoever broke early had to, for one day, come in with a ridiculous moustache as their penance. I had that day skillfully shaped my remaining whiskers into what is known as a "horseshoe"—one grown with extensions down the sides of my mouth—to announce my defeat. To be honest, it made me look like someone who without question had on an ankle bracelet and by law shouldn't be within 500 yards of an elementary school. Little did I know my upper lip accoutrement would be the least of my problems when this picture came back to haunt us.

We said our good-byes and headed for home. I had taken the rest of the day off from work due to an "extenuating circumstance." It was a long trek though, and I began to second-guess my decision to drive so far with the horse's head prominently displayed to any motorists unfortunate enough to follow us. At one point I even pulled over and respectfully covered its face with a plastic bag thinking it would reduce the gruesomeness of the spectacle. Instead, it transformed something already mildly creepy into a much, much worse show of horror.

Seeing its long-nosed facial expression so suffocatingly fixed from beneath the plastic, it really hinted at something fiendish transpiring, possibly even with overtones of bestiality or other unhealthy sexual ambitions. Cole, with total agreement from me, yanked the bag and we continued on our way with fingers crossed.

Unfortunately, on the way out of town, I heard the wail of a siren and saw flashing blue lights in my rearview mirror. I pulled over and a state trooper strutted up to the driver's side window, with his chest puffed out and campaign hat pulled down low to just above his eyes.

"What seems to be the problem, officer?" I asked coyly.

"Well, you could start by telling me what you're doing with a moose out of season," he said. Poaching is a serious offense in the Greatland, a sacrilege really, and I could tell this lawman was ready and eager to write me a litany of citations.

"I don't mean to tell you your business, officer, but that's not a moose."

"What do you mean it's not a moose? I just walked past—" he stopped in midsentence while staring at the rounded hooves of the horse, rather than cloven ones of a moose. He scanned the rest of the corpse and when I saw his head snap backwards practically off his shoulders, I knew he had registered the mistake. He said nothing more than "have a nice day," before heading back to his cruiser.

IT WAS OUR FIRST HORSE, BUT FAR FROM OUR LAST. EACH AND EVERY equine donation that followed presented its own unique set of problems to overcome and backbreaking work to endure, but the money saved and the dogs' satisfaction made it worth the effort. In fact, the only time I have ever regretted doing anything with a dead horse came a few months after I posted the picture of that first triumph.

Over the years and as Cole's fan base grew to include folks from all around the world, the photos we've posted on our blog began to bring in mixed reviews from strangers. Internet anonymity often means people aren't scared to pull their punches when it comes to letting you know *exactly* how they feel about an issue, and no subject was more controversial than our harvesting of horse meat.

Some people who had horses or—as was often synonymous, lived lifestyles where butchering livestock was a common occurrence—wrote to pass on praise for making the most out of a sad situation. Others respectfully wrote to say that while they could never bloody their own hands butchering an animal themselves, they acknowledged the undesirable process was how meat got to their tables, and they understood why someone else wouldn't want to waste a half ton of meat.

Still others—which we learned from their Internet profiles were mostly very young people, or those living a completely urbanized lifestyle where beef, pork, and chicken were known only as neatly packaged products from the grocery store—would write to tell us, in loquacious detail, what horrible people we are.

I don't know what any of them looked like, but from the diatribes they sent, I could imagine their sour faces, and practically feel the heat of anger with which they hammered out their polemics on the keyboard. And to be honest, their e-mails initially stymied more than angered me.

Most horses we hauled back to the kennel had died of old age, or, by their owners' hand as a result of some geriatric condition that caused them to no longer have a pleasant quality of life. One or two had also been accidental deaths, such as a horse breaking its neck after running into a fence when something spooked it. We have *never*, and I mean *ever*, personally killed any of the horses.

So it came as a complete shock to me when one morning while checking a social media site, I clicked on a link a friend sent me with the comment "WTF?!" underneath it. This brought me to a site offering "Texas Horse Hunting," which to be clear was not advertising hunting by horseback, but actually hunting and killing horses with, as the site stated, "sticks, clubs, or crossbows."

With the exception of, say, gas station sandwiches, where the egg salad has shifted color from a delicious yellow to a suspicious gray, few things could make my stomach churn like someone bludgeoning a living horse for sport. But what sent waves of nausea rolling through me and set my jaw to clenching so tightly I nearly ground my teeth to powder was when I realized the site's cover picture of "satisfied customers" was Cole and me and the young couple from the day we loaded the horse into the pickup.

"NOOOOOOOO!" I shouted involuntarily, bringing Cole sprinting downstairs to check if I'd suffered a stroke, or had resumed my morning interest in primal scream therapy.

I couldn't believe the depravity I was seeing advertised next to a photo of my smiling face, and became more enraged the further into the site I read. Not only had my photo been plagiarized—a serious criminal offense against a freelance journalist like myself—but it was also being used cosmically far out of context.

Words like "intellectual property theft," "copyright infringement," and "defamation of character," began to rattle around in my frontal lobe, but that train of thought was broken when a call from the local 4-H chapter came in after making its way indirectly from the national and state chapter offices. That awkward exchange, from my end, went something like this:

"No, we don't hunt horses."

"Yes, it was my idea to take the picture."

"No, I'm not a sadist."

"Yes, I understand my wife is wearing a 4-H sweatshirt and that causes problems for you."

"No, I don't have an easy-for-you-to-understand explanation for why we're smiling."

"Yes, we promise to not pose for any more photos with expired equines while wearing 4-H apparel."

With that dispiriting call concluded, I returned to researching the site, and deduced it to be a satirical hoax, one I speculated was created by teens somewhere who had simply stumbled onto our photo while surfing the net.

Still, we couldn't let this slandering stand, so I contacted Google and—after proving ownership of the photo and how it was being misused—got them to remove it from the website. We also contacted Snopes.com, a myth-debunking site, and had them help invalidate the false assumption created by the photo being used, but the electrical cauterizing to slow this disease's progression was more difficult than these few steps.

Facebook had to be contacted to report the photo as harmful each time it is forwarded and shared, as well as contacting those sharing it. That, I found, was one of the hardest parts. Two of the Facebook pages where the photo spread the fastest were "Anti-Hunting in America" and "The Barking Army."

The former of the two responded quickly after I wrote them and proved the falsehood of the photo, yet it still was shared 66 times before the post was removed and a correction posted. The latter site was more resistant, as were its followers. They posted a correction with a link to our real blog and website, where *actual* animal welfare work is done, but they left up the phony photo and link. Over the first twenty-four hours the hoax photo was shared 255 times and brought in hundreds of hurtful comments (many revolving around my horseshoe mustache, stating how anyone who would flaunt one likely not only derived sexual gratification from hurting animals, but also in feverishly copulating with their sister or other siblings). Meanwhile, the real link to our own site brought in two shares, no positive comments, and $0 in donations to help feed and house real rescued dogs.

It was irksome to realize that the same people who were so outraged when they thought the animal abuse was real had little to say—and zero to donate—when they found out their moral misjudgment. Cole and I never asked for praise for our efforts to help animals, but an acknowledgment from those who'd rushed to judge us—that their misplaced criticisms could have damaged our ability to continue to do so—would have been nice.

The irony of this character assassination was perhaps the most hurtful part, though. At that point in our lives, Cole and I had taken in more than forty dogs, much to our own financial detriment, but working toward the humane treatment and protection of animals was nothing new to either of us.

Prior to coming to Alaska, Cole and I were zoologists and zookeepers for nearly a decade, working with threatened and endangered animals at well-respected institutions such as the Wildlife Conservation Society. In our twenties, I traipsed through cobra-infested fields in Sri Lanka during one of the bloodiest times of their civil war in an effort to track and protect native primate species. Cole, as a single American woman, risked her own safety walking antipoaching patrols in the savannas of Kenya to ensure the protection of black rhinos in Africa.

I consider myself an animal rights activist, but there's a difference between activist—actively living in service to the betterment of animals—and extremist, whose greatest activity involves spouting off loud, vitriolic lip service to the cause. I remember this latter group from high school, college, and beyond, often eager to run their mouths, but not nearly as eager to do the real work—as I did—of volunteering at the local no-kill animal shelter or heading to the field to save animals in situ. And apparently now that they are grown up they are much the same, but rather than just making bumper stickers and T-shirts, they now use social media as their weapon of choice and carpet bomb us with their ideals.

WHILE STOMPING OUT THAT INTERNET WILDFIRE WAS NOT SOON forgotten, another horse incident was even more memorable, in part because the call came in on Christmas Day. It was an older animal that had apparently succumbed to the below-freezing temperatures at that time.

Spending Christmas morning opening a horse's abdominal cavity, rather than presents, wasn't exactly what Cole and I were hoping for, but as I already stated, a horse is too much free meat to pass up, so we threw on our snow boots and winter clothes and picked up the horse carcass. It was an uneventful donation. The horse's owner seemed as eager to get back to his seasonal festivities as we were, and he met us at the end of his driveway with the horse in the front-loader bucket of a tractor. He just lowered it into the bed of our pickup.

Back at home, we realized, like most old horses that die in winter, he didn't have a ton of meat on him. Many give up the ghost during the cold-weather months because their teeth have worn down to the point where it's tough for them to grind enough hay and other feed to keep sufficient weight on to burn the calories needed to survive the harsh and prolonged drop in temperature.

Not wanting to squander our Yule time together by butchering all day, we decided to just leave the main carcass in the bed of the truck, and merely take the edible organs out and quarter the old nag. Our intent was to finish the bulk of skinning and carving meat from the bone the next day.

We should have checked the weather first.

That night the mercury plummeted into the deep minuses, thirty below at least. When we woke up the next morning ready to work we found not only were all the horse parts we had left in the bed completely cold petrified to a near-granite hardness, but also all the blood that pooled an inch deep the day before had frozen and welded everything to the bed itself.

We decided to try to chisel the largest pieces loose by using a sledgehammer to knock a maul head like a large wedge. I threw my coat down and hiked up the suspenders of my insulated bibs, and began swinging like a maniacal miner.

Fifteen minutes later, my cheeks were rosy, my brow sweaty, I was panting like an asthmatic with a misplaced inhaler, and worst of all I had nothing—not one stinking piece of flash-frozen horse—to show for it. Cole—six months pregnant at the time—and I took turns over the next hour or so. We each swung the maul to the point of exhaustion, which only amounted to sending a few port-colored shards of shattered blood-sickles flying in all directions, much to the glee of our mooching house dogs that were circling the truck like sharks.

We needed a new plan. We decided rather than killing ourselves we would just wait for it to warm up a bit, and hopefully the carcass would soften enough for us to make a dent in it, figuratively and literally. We gave it a few days.

Oh, what a terrible plan this was.

Every time we let out the house dogs to play or relieve themselves, they immediately honed in on the carcass, jumping into the bed of the truck and kibbling and gnawing whatever they could greedily choke back before a flustered Cole or I would run them off. Worse still, the carcass chummed in an orgy of birds, everything from shrieking magpies and scores of ravens to the occasional bald eagle, and not only did they each peck and bite a few beakfuls, but they began shitting all over my truck and the carcass itself. The truck bed became streaked in revolting white fecal ribbons that gave it an appearance somewhat between an Alfred Hitchcock horror flick and a Jackson Pollock masterpiece.

Something had to be done. By the end of the first week, the dogs and the birds had annihilated all meat from the carcass. It basically became just a pile of bones, hide, and a jagged substrate of blood-ice. We resorted back to our original plan, but this time we employed the youthful stamina of our niece and nephew, and over the course of a weekend, we each took turns excavating what remained of the equine cadaver. It took the full two days and a lot of arduous effort, but we finally freed all the frozen parts of the horse from the bed.

With a sigh of relief, we were ready to finally take what had affectionately come to be known as "The Hoofed Horror Show" to the dump, and just in the nick of time. The extended weather forecast called for some heavy accumulations and the first flurries were starting to fall about the time we finished. I slid behind the wheel of my pickup, inserted the key, and turned the ignition, only to be met with the sound of silence.

And not the soothing Simon and Garfunkel kind. It was the horrible, soul-crushing kind of quiet that instantly told me this carcass was going to be with us for a bit longer.

In all the chaos to clean our self-made mess, I had completely forgotten to plug the truck in during the minus temperatures. The battery—and my morale, for that matter—were as dead as the horse.

The beastly remains, buried beneath several inches of the heavy, wet snow, ended up staying there till the season changed, giving new meaning to the term "spring cleaning" when the weather finally did warm and I repaired the truck enough to make a run to the local landfill. Looking back on that horse, I can honestly say it was the worst Christmas present I ever received.

The Religion of Dog

HALFWAY TO MY TURNAROUND POINT, THE TOP OF THE 2,860-foot Ptarmigan Peak—the highest point in the Caribou Hills—I began to realize my mistake with testicle-shriveling certainty. The wind picked up to a steady twenty miles per hour, with occasional stronger gusts that would yank my hooded ruff down over my face and nearly knock me off the sled. Rather than falling from the sky, a heavy, wet snow horizontally hurled itself at us, and every time we took a turn that angled us directly into the teeth of the gale, the exposed skin of my face felt a blast like taking pellets from an ice-loaded shotgun.

Mushing, particularly in extreme inclement weather, is somewhat like poker if you envision you're playing against Mother Nature and gambling with your life. With stakes so high, it's essential to have dogs you can truly count on, especially at the front end of the team, and on this day I went all-in to find out if mine were good enough to beat the odds.

Even utter novices to the sport of mushing still have an awareness of the term "lead dog," but there is so much more to a leader than running in front of the team. That's not to say there aren't dogs that will lead from time to time for brief stints, but these are not true lead dogs. Not the type that at 800 to 900 miles into a race and feeling fatigued will still stand up, shake off their stiffness, and not only begin to pull, but

Cyder, a thick-bodied and barrel-chested male, displayed awe-inspiring athletic abilities for charging through deep powder.

sometimes literally drag the other dogs out of a checkpoint with them.

Having to run just a little harder and faster to keep the gangline taught, sometimes breaking trail, never reaping the benefit of the wake from a dog in front of you—the lead position is physically and mentally demanding. Only a small percentage of all sled dogs are suited for it, and fewer still will be the type of leader that when pressed can steadfastly do it mile after mile, year after year, in any conditions.

In our kennel, we have been blessed to have a handful of extraordinarily reliable leaders, and deciding which dogs take the position out front is often dictated by weather or state of the trail, and like a race, may change at a moment's notice. Penny, a wheat-colored, twenty-five-pound female, the size and build of a whippet, has an indomitable drive and shines late in races when other dogs may be too tired to motivate off of their comfy straw beds. Oaky, a muscular, forty-pound, cream-colored female, is fantastic at the start of races due to her ability to follow commands and turn on a dime when speeds are high and missing a turn could mean losing several minutes and positions in the standings. But in storms where the wind is serious enough to slap a grown man to the ground, or snow falls in heaping feet rather than a few inches, we sometimes need larger dogs, and we'll turn to the juggernauts of the kennel.

Cyder and Zoom stand out in our kennel as the heavy artillery, only marched to the front lines when at war with the worst of winter elements. Their unflappable athletic abilities, aptitude for adhering to even the most obliterated trail, and natural large sizes make them a dynamic duo when running out front of a long string of dogs.

Cyder is as stalwart a dog as I have ever seen and the canine equivalent of an NFL linebacker—a huge, seventy-five-pound, thick-bodied and barrel-chested male. He has half-pricked ears and bleached-blue eyes that relay his always serious attitude about life. His pelage coloring is two-toned, with most of his body bearing a dark cinnamon color, while his undersides and mask blend to more of a tangerine shade, and eventually give way to white on his muzzle and paws. He stoically runs, no matter the temperature, the depth of the snow, the bite of the wind; he is always ready to move forward. Cyder isn't as fast as some of the lighter-boned dogs, but he stays as steady as a metronome in lead and always achieves the goal with uncompromised resolve.

Zoom is Cyder's female equivalent in size, tipping the scales to seventy pounds, *very* large for her gender. Her eyes are also as light and blue as two pools of water, but have an almost Egyptian-like liner of thick black

Zoom, a few weeks old and her eyes just starting to open. We couldn't have known then this tiny pup would grow into such a dynamo.

bordering them. Her floppy ears also have this attractive, pencil-thin black trim to their edges. They, along with the top of her head, back saddle, and tail, are a washed-out ochre color, while not just her muzzle, but her whole face is polar white, matching her chest, underbelly, and legs.

She too is herculean in her strength, but that is where the similarities between the two end. Zoom's personality is distinctly different in that she has always been a highly excitable dog, much like her mother who was appropriately named A.D. for Attention Deficit. She has more of a high-pitched chirp than a bark, and any sign of possibly running sets her off, from moving a four-wheeler, to pulling out a harness, to starting the dog truck—she will go nuts sounding more like a robin defending its nest than a sled dog ready to pull.

Zoom likes traveling to unknown places and meeting new people, so race starts at which she can jump on, lick, and generally accost total strangers are always fun times for her. I've often thought if Zoom were a person, she would likely be the head of an office party-planning committee somewhere.

When actually in race mode, we always have to work hard to keep Zoom from expending too much energy while waiting in the starting chute as the clock counts down. She'll chirp, spume at the mouth, and lunge out trying to join each passing team until it's her turn. Once out of the chute, Zoom blazes trail in an almost effortless fashion, a skill she's displayed since roughly a year old. Leading has always come naturally to her.

The true hero is flawed, however, and like the locks of Samson and the heel of Achilles, these behemoth dogs are not without their imperfections. Zoom's downside relates to rises in mercury. A true "Alaskan" husky, she is prone to overheating while working in warm daytime temperatures, so we tend to use her in lead mostly for night runs.

Cyder's weakness is an almost clinical case of xenophobia— a crippling fear of strangers. If not for the inconvenience, it would practically be comical to watch the ends this brawny and typically dutiful dog will go to avoid contact with anyone he doesn't know. Race starts swelling with people, crowded checkpoints, and finish lines loaded with onlookers are thoroughly terrifying to him. Cole has lost minutes in races where upon approaching a checkpoint, Cyder spotted someone shifting in the distance and dashed off the trail, ducked for cover in the trees, or simply came to a halt.

These two shortcomings are easy to overlook when compared against their strengths though. I recall Cole telling me one of their shining moments from her first Iditarod. Teams struggled to not become mired in nearly waist-deep snow. After hours of slogging through a narrow trail in the forest, Cole and the dogs found themselves facing a new challenge—a large open expanse, possibly a lake or marsh in the warmer months, but in that weather it appeared as a smooth white quilt of snow.

Zoom, the white-faced, blue-eyed dog on the left, was large for a female and highly excitable. She could generate, and motivate, a lot of forward momentum when partnered with Cyder.

The winds, a stronger force to contend with once out from the protection of trees, also must have blown down or buried the markers. With no tracks or trails from other teams in front of Cole, she had no idea which direction to head when crossing the area to pick up an unseen trail in the woods on the other side.

In these conditions, it's all up to the lead dogs, which can somehow smell the faint scent of where another team has traveled through the deep powder. Other times the dogs sense through their paws slight differences in the density of the snow—the subtle feel of a harder pack where a trail once was—and they do it in a way a musher never could through their thick boots. They have an almost sixth sense for detecting muted clues.

Cyder and Zoom knew what to do without Cole asking when they all found themselves in the great white nothing. They bounded through the snow, their heads and shoulders occasionally visible when they would porpoise up, 80 feet away from Cole. She called, "Gee. Gee. Gee," their command to keep turning right, hoping they would eventually turn until they felt the trail, but 360 degrees later, they hadn't picked up on anything. They had merely stamped down a circle with a 160-foot diameter, risking life-threatening tangles in the process since the gangline is not forgiving to the slack that can come from these kinds of maneuvers.

They began to make the huge circle again, when suddenly Cyder and Zoom must have caught a hint of something different this time. Their demeanor changed, suddenly more confident, and they began to plow forward. Trusting their lead, Cole eventually began to see markers once again when they neared the woods on the far side. Cyder and Zoom, like always, had found the correct trail.

I already alluded to one of my own fondest memories of these two charging headlong to *make* a trail that grim day in the Caribou Hills, a range of mountains not far from our home. If this area were a letter, it would be a capital *R*. It is remote, rugged, and its beauty rare and rejuvenating to the soul. It is raw, the hills are relentless, and in a raging storm like I found myself this day with Cyder and Zoom, even an atheist could find religion.

Far from the nearest road system, the area was once without signs or markers anywhere, and the only way to learn the landscape was to venture through enough times with someone who already knew it. Slowly over time, you grow accustomed to traveling through the gulches and valleys, begin to recognize the smooth contours of cornices, and find hints of familiarity in the serpent-like twists and turns of the trails.

The section I was mushing in is locally referred to as the "high country." As the name implies, the trails skirt the clouds, high above tree line and miles from any safety cabins or the possibility of cell phone reception. Moonlike, there are few features to use for bearings among the miles of smooth, undulating hills of white in every direction. Snow accumulates at great depths here due to the presence of an adjacent 700-square-mile contiguous ice field. The deep powder can be challenging enough, but the high altitude also means that even a moderate wind can dramatically move snow, displacing or depositing several feet in a matter of minutes.

The weather in this area is always schizophrenic, frequently doling out the chance to experience all four seasons over the course of a six-hour run, and this day, a bout of manic aggressive behavior appeared to be building. On the horizon loomed a storm, with menacingly dark, dull clouds sagging low enough to swallow the hilltops that lay ahead of me.

Roughly halfway into the run, the last sign of life I bore witness to transpired more than an hour earlier. Prior to climbing above the last stands of spruce and willow, I accidently flushed a covey of pearl white ptarmigan. They shrieked shrilly before flying away into a thick fog, where they dematerialized into the featureless ghostly mist and left me alone and in a silence broken only by the swish of the sled's runners and the soft, rhythmic panting of the dogs' breaths.

Believing I had come too far to turn around, and knowing that it's good to expose the dogs to a little wind and inclement weather so they learn to overcome these hurdles when they eventually face them in a race, I pulled the zipper of my parka up to my chin and thought, *Some "storm training" would be good for the gang.* I convinced myself that if I moved swiftly, I could get in and out of the high country before things got too dangerous.

I was wrong.

Nearing Ptarmigan Peak, with the snow assailing and the wind stabbing, my confidence in the decision to press forward commenced to crack like a dry log under a heavy maul. Despite my hands being deep in my beaver mittens, my fingers ached. Inside my astronaut-sized boots my toes were numb. My chin was pressed so far into my neck they became one with the exception of when I glanced over my shoulder to see the trail behind us closing as quickly as we put it in. I knew if we could even make it to the turnaround—a teardrop loop around the peak's summit cone—we would be plowing our way back home.

At the front of the team I could see Cyder and Zoom, but just barely. They both had their noses down and were leaning heavily into their har-

Breaking trail with the dogs in snow nearly as deep as they were tall. A few miles farther up the trail from where this picture was taken, accumulated snow piled to a depth over their heads, but they still plowed forward.

nesses like two broad-shouldered oxen trying to break a stuck plow free. The snow on the trail, initially just a few inches thick, was starting to build to depths nearly as high as the dogs were tall. It slowed their momentum, and while they plodded forward, neither Cyder nor Zoom ever looked back for my reassurance. They knew they had a job to do and they weren't just doing it, they were doing it well. They made gees and haws as I called them out, but there was no trail to follow. I directed from my memory, more than by sight, since I could see next to nothing.

Somehow, astonishingly, we made it to the halfway point and turned around, but then our roles reversed. I became a passenger rather than the driver of my dog-powered vehicle. The snow was blinding. I squinted and strained to see where we were, trying to glean any knowledge of our current location.

The visibility for the dogs was worse. Occasionally, I had to stop and wade to the front of the team to wipe the caked snow from Cyder and Zoom's eyelashes. Getting there and back was exhausting in the deep powder, and left me soaked down to my synthetic long johns. Also, each time I returned to the sled, I would be near the point of hyperventilating, with the cold air acting like an icy rasp, filing my throat and burning my lungs.

In this monochrome world, with no way to tell where the sky ended and the ground began, I sensed more than saw the shapes and contours of the terrain. I felt my way along blindly, experiencing a stomach-in-the-throat sensation when plunging down snow dunes, and vertigo from leaning into serpentine curves of the trail. The presence of the unseen unnerved me the farther we traveled. It was like riding a roller coaster—albeit a sluggish one—with my eyes closed.

The wail of the savage winds devoured all sounds, including any commands to the front of the team, and the snow—getting deeper and deeper—felt on the verge of swallowing us. Even the dogs had a cupcake-thick icing of white to their fur. I began to feel not just lonely, but very *only*—the only one brave enough, the only one stupid enough, the only one to be mushing on a mountaintop miles from any other humans. Even the ptarmigan I had seen hours before had the sense to stick together.

My Plan B entailed always making sure Plan A was bulletproof, but

Cole and her team near the cliff at the "End of the World" on a clear weather day. Not nearly as pleasant when I perilously mushed a team past this panorama during a hellacious high-country storm.

I needed to start considering my alternatives. I mulled the idea of ducking for cover down in a gulley out of the full force of the wind, so I leaned over the sled bow and unzipped the sled bag slightly in order to mentally reassure myself by inventorying my supplies. I had my emergency duffel in the sled with some basic survival items: a flare, sleeping bag, cooker, and a sack of kibble.

However, there were no tea leaves at the bottom telling me what the future held or quelling the uncertainties billowing in my brain. In the raging tempest tearing away at us, trying to use any of the gear I brought seemed unfeasible, plus, storms in this area could last for a day or more. I knew if the dogs and I weren't back at our own den by nightfall Cole would be worried, and if we weren't home by morning she would be sending out a search-and-rescue team.

Distressed, I decided to keep moving, but an even more uneasy feeling began to gnaw deep at my insides because I knew our return entailed traversing back across an area very appropriately called the "End of the World." It ran right alongside the lip of a near-vertical cliff overlooking a valley at the bottom of which was nestled the headwaters of glacially fed Tustumena Lake, Alaska's eighth largest. It had been a sketchy undertaking crossing this wide-open area on the way out, but I began to wonder if on the return the dogs would be able to sniff out the trail we had put in, or if we would go over the edge and free-fall to the valley floor several thousand feet below.

My life, all our lives, were in Cyder and Zoom's paws.

It was a surreal experience, surrendering my control and putting all my trust in my canine companions. As children we frequently relinquish our fears to someone older and wiser. We launch out of a swing at its zenith to fly through the air because we know if we get hurt mom will put a bandage on the wound. We sleep soundly at night despite our initial fright for what may have lurked under the bed because dad checked it and gave his reassurance all was clear. As we get older we continue to rely on other humans for our safety and security. Our husbands and wives will protect us from heartbreak, doctors will cure us when we're ill, police will come when we're in danger. But all of these scenarios entail putting our faith, our complete faith, in another human being.

And, when all else fails, we turn to religion and hope God will protect us from harm in whatever way these other humans fell short. Rare are the circumstances in which we, the supposedly apex species of the planet, rely on another creature for our immediate survival. However, at that moment, in a raging mountaintop blizzard, it was another three-letter being that I put all my faith in: D-O-G.

In my torpid state, the blood in my veins feeling like chilled molasses, I literally did nothing but hold on, relying on this dynamic duo's memories and counting on the power of their ancestral instincts to take over. I watched in as much awe as admiration as Cyder and Zoom led the way using some ethereal understanding of the frozen windswept landscape. The rest of the team snaked behind them as they plowed a two-dog-wide mini-canyon through the powder.

Their shoulders moved up and down like pistons, taking exaggeratedly high steps to contend with the deep drifts. They seemed mechanical, moving forward without any outward signs of fear or hesitation. Theoretically the driver, I reverently stood at the back as a passenger. My sole action was shivering, violently. More a series of shudders, really, that built one after another from deep within me—partially from cold partially from fear—until my teeth banged together and my whole body twitched.

I could see nothing except for the dogs themselves. Everything else gone, swallowed in white. No way to tell our location or speed. My entire world was featureless negative space, a colorless vortex, which the dogs cleaved through. This went on for miles, and what seemed like hours, before we finally started to drop down in elevation, escaping the brunt of the storm. I began to see familiar landmarks faintly appear like a darkroom photograph as we slowly descended, back to the cover of trees, and the security of recognizable trail. Quickly gone were the screams of wind and the blowing snow that penetrated every seam of my clothing, and deepest recesses of my mind.

We made it through with only my parka and nerves a bit worse for the wear. I became filled with the first warm feelings in hours, swelling from thankfulness that we all survived. To me a life-changing experience had occurred. A bond forged between man and animal that few will ever know. We had faced some of the worst nature could throw at us and came through it together. I set the hooks and ran to the front of the team to give Cyder and Zoom a big hug, and as I wrapped my puffy-coated arms around their broad chests, the expression on their faces surprised me.

Neither acted like anything out of the ordinary had happened. Cyder used the break to gulp down big mouthfuls of snow, while Zoom did her usual thing, giving me big, wet licks for kneeling so close to her. I couldn't help but laugh, and count my blessings. To them it had been nothing, but to me they had been everything. They never lost heart, and in turn my own filled with commensurate admiration for their heroic deeds.

Some say fate holds all the cards and that may be so, but Cyder and Zoom were the king and queen of my kennel's deck on many occasions and on that day they were also definitely my ace in the hole. Perhaps, for putting us in that predicament, that made me the joker; I'm not sure.

What I do know for certain is that there are moments in time that resonate, staying with you forever. For me, that infamous training run stands out as one of them. I glimpsed divinity and understood—possibly for the first time at that spiritual depth—the perfection embodied in Cyder and Zoom. I appreciated, truly, the caliber of athletic performance they emanated. I valued the privilege of not just knowing a once-in-a-musher's-lifetime lead dog, but knowing two of them.

Shit Outta Luck

W E'RE ALMOST IN THE CLEAR, I THOUGHT AS I NERVOUSLY checked my watch for the 600th time during the hour-long puppy socialization class and realized we only had fifteen minutes to go. I had been trying my best to disassociate from the insanity of corralling our seven husky puppies that by comparison to all the pampered purebreds were acting certifiably insane.

Cole did most of the legwork—as well as receiving of hard stares and conspicuously audible guffaws from the human participants—while I blended into the wall between the rack of heavily-fingered *Dog Fancy* magazines and the dozens of 8 by 10 portraits of pets and middle-aged women holding up various colored ribbons with a giddy enthusiasm usually reserved for lottery winners.

We knew going into the class we didn't want any undesignated deposits, so we had foregone feeding the pups since breakfast, more than eight hours earlier. We also dutifully walked them before and obsessively during the class. I was just about to start leaning back on my heels when a woman whose formal wardrobe suggested she served as president of her own one-woman Jane Austen fan club apprised me of the gravity of the situation. She had caught my eye moments earlier by amorously smooching her Cavalier King Charles spaniel, but her gelid gasp now commanded the room's attention.

I followed her gaze to one of our pups: Buckwheat—a fuzzy, custard-colored male with honey eyes. It took me a second to figure out why he had garnished the spotlight any more than his littermates who were fanned out and a-little-too-merrily making mischief around the room—from pinning down other pups to chewing on the agility obstacles. Then I recognized Buckwheat's posture as unmistakably preparing to poop: rear legs spread wide, front legs stiff and pulled in close, and his whole body arched into a pushing hunch.

"Houston, we have a problem," I mumbled to myself.

Knowing the mess coming down the pike, I felt immediate tension, like the kind when finding a note from the boss at 5:00 P.M. on a Friday that reads "We need to talk on Monday." I knew nothing good was to follow.

All dog owners probably have a story or two about a dog leaving a tightly coiled pile somewhere they shouldn't have, and over the years we've had more than our fair share of accidents in the house, truck, shoes, and numerous other unwanted places. At the time they're happening, they are *never* funny. But, looking back on the incidents, some of the messiest and most bowel-clearing blasts that we've suffered through are now some of our most, dare I say, effervescent memories with our dogs.

Not everyone could see the humor in our huskies pooping at an inappropriate time, though. Case in point, all the people whose faces puckered into tart expressions when Buckwheat sabotaged their puppy socialization class. This day's event was no informal gathering of mutts, which should have been enough to dissuade us, but no, we rolled the dice and literally crapped out during one of the rare times we attempted to cross into the world of purebred dogdom, and attended an American Kennel Club event.

Despite the fact that mushers, agility enthusiasts, and those who partake in obedience or conformation are all dog lovers, there seems to be a large cultural rift separating the former from these latter groups. I don't profess to fully understanding this whole doggy dynamic. Suffice to say,

Buckwheat at or around the age when he embarrassingly lost control of his bowels during a puppy socialization class. At the time incontinence incidents are occurring, they're never funny, but I've found that the bigger the mess, the longer the memories linger.

though, Cole and I were blissfully unaware of this elitism in the world of animal lovers when we enrolled in the class, but like learning there are dogs with registered names longer than my own, I found the experience acerbically educational.

We signed up shortly after our core race dogs—Butterscotch, a tangerine-colored female, and, Doc, a snow-white husky with dazzling blue eyes—produced the first litter of puppies in our kennel. Until then the bulk of our brood consisted of dogs and puppies adopted from other people and the pound, and nearly all displayed troublesome idiosyncrasies in varying degrees. Our thought was, by lovingly raising a litter ourselves, we could infuse these well-mannered new additions into the kennel and establish a new level of normality.

Their behavior in the class quickly made me realize "normal" is a subjective term.

In my defense, I called ahead to make sure it would be OK to bring in our litter, since there were seven of them after all. All puppies have a reputation for kinetics, but huskies are in a league of their own. They're like cans of energy drink come to life.

"Fine, it's totally fine," the instructor assured me with a pedestrian tone when I called the day before. "We've had hundreds of puppies come through. I'm sure there isn't anything your dogs could do that would be something we haven't seen in class before."

She even mentioned their punch-card system, and since we were bringing so many pups, we should consider getting one for this, and future, rendezvous. We figured we should see how it went first.

Arriving, we initially felt on edge, but walking into the playroom I began to wonder if all our worries had been for nothing. The air was rich with the distinct and charming scent of cedar, possibly from the bedding material in several of the carrier-kennels the other pups in the class had been transported in. The room was the size of a basketball court with various pieces of doggy furniture—mainly agility obstacles like weave poles and soft-fabric tunnels—scattered around for the dogs to play in. Underfoot, from corner to corner and wall to wall, were soft, gym-like, black rubber mats covering the entire floor space. I couldn't say for certain at the time, but the mats seemed water- (or more specifically, urine-) proof. We soon found out they were that and then some.

I should preface this part of the story by explaining some extenuating circumstances. A few weeks prior, we had received the disheartening diagnosis that Buckwheat had a liver shunt. Without getting too scientific, this condition causes a blood vessel to transport blood *around* instead of through the liver, where it can be purified. As a result, byproducts of proteins—such as from digestion of dog food—build up in the bloodstream and become toxic. Buckwheat's treatment required him to eat a special diet and take medication, both of which gave him extremely viscous stools, completely deficient in color.

Once I realized Buckwheat was about to have the most public of all accidents, I totally froze in fear and just stood there. I'm not proud of it, but to be fair, I could tell by how far along Buckwheat's anus was dilated, we were going to need a miracle to change the situation and you really don't want to be sitting down when hoping to suddenly pull a miracle out of your ass.

Cole, being the pragmatist of the two of us, made a dash for him, but hadn't even crossed half the room when nothing short of an anal outpouring began spilling out of Buckwheat's backside.

To be honest, I'm certain had any dog dropped a deuce in the class it would have been frowned upon, and it didn't help that the stink of his stool, for some odd reason, smelled like we had fed him a strict diet of cheap cigars. But what really made the folks in the room go from looking down their noses at us to scooping up their puppies and running out in sheer terror was the appearance of Buckwheat's stool. It came out ghastly white, with a consistency more liquid than anything close to a solid state, like a bottle of knocked over milk, glug, glug, glugging its way to emptiness.

I think parents on a beach where someone has pointed at the water and screamed "Shark!" have moved slower than these pet owners did. Shih-tzus were snatched up in seconds. A completely unathletic woman made an Olympic-caliber lunge for her Lhasa apsos, while another frantically scooped up her bichon frise. Dogs in hand, they fled posthaste.

I couldn't blame them. Without knowing Buckwheat's condition, his deluge of defecation bore such an unusual appearance, had he not been ours, I likely would have thought him the harbinger of a horrible virus and ran out of there in an act of puppy preservation, too.

Slouch-shouldered and with head held low, I tried to placate the instructor with sincere apologies. "We're sorry, so, so sorry," I said.

"It happens," she replied, stone-faced, while handing me a roll of paper towels and a spray bottle of disinfectant.

We never inquired about the punch card.

. . .

BUCKWHEAT ASS-BLASTING THE CLASS WAS ONE OF OUR MOST EMBAR-rassing moments, but far from the most shocking. That incident began with a free-range bird we had cooked for a Thanksgiving feast, the left-overs of which proved too tempting for Tatika, our German shepherd, to leave alone.

Tatika embodied all the textbook traits of her breed. She was black-and-tan, large in size, a devoted protector, and resolutely disciplined. Typically, had a plate of steak been placed on the floor in front of her, unless given the green light, she wouldn't so much as steal a sniff.

When it came to wild game, however, all bets were off. There must have been a different smell, a scent that triggered something primitive buried deep in her genes. It always proved too tantalizing for her to resist, and when she broke, she binged.

We went back to work the day after the holiday, and mistakenly left Tatika home alone with the golden-brown bird sitting in a pan of its suc-culent juices on the stove. I can only wonder how long it took till she broke, but when we returned, the empty oven top was clear evidence that I would not be enjoying days of turkey melts, turkey enchiladas, and the numerous other leftovers I annually looked forward to.

The living room and kitchen were clean. Tatika had hid her crime well, but I followed my nose and walked farther back in the house toward our sleeping quarters, where a wafting scent—like that of a rotisserie—became overwhelming.

I apprehensively entered the bedroom, afraid of what I might find. Our bed had always been one of Tatika's favorite locales to rest and chew on toys during the day while waiting for us to get home, and on more than one occasion I wilted at finding a thick puddle of shampoo waiting for me as she also enjoyed taking the caps off bottles from the bathroom.

This was far worse.

By the time we had ended our eight-hour shifts, there remained only a few spindly bones and jagged chips left on our pillows. The comforter and sheets—from where she must have struggled to grip the carcass between her paws while working in it—looked like they had been greased with butter. They were wet, shiny, giant Rorschach blotches of bird juice.

We didn't even try to clean them. We knew better. Utterly saturated and soaked through with the bird's natural fatty oils, we stripped the bed and threw everything away.

Despite what a mess she made, the real chaos came the next day as the pounds of rich white and dark meat wreaked havoc on Tatika's digestive processes. Normally, even when coming home late (which we weren't), Tatika showed such discipline that she could, and I think would, hold it until her colon collapsed under the pressure. But this was not a normal situation.

Rather than greeting us, she nearly knocked us down as she blew past us. Instead of heading to the woods where she religiously relieved herself, she stopped a few feet from us and immediately pooped on the lawn. Knowing how much she had ingested twenty-four hours earlier, I peeked in, not entirely sure how horrific today's mess would be. I recoiled at the sight of excrement to the extreme, and uttered the two most appropriate words ever spoken.

"Holy shit!"

On the rare occasions Tatika did have an accident in the house, it was usually right by the front door. She would then be so embarrassed, she would put as much distance between herself and the accident as possible, and hide in the laundry room or our back bedroom.

This literal shit-storm, far more than one pile and too large to constrain to one area, gave off a stench like a sewer main had burst. There were grisly smears, not only in our bedroom, but also in the laundry room, back bedroom, at the front door, in the living room and kitchen, and in several places in-between where she must have been going while panicking to find a spot she hadn't already coated in large brown splatters of explosive diarrhea. Even our bed, again, had been sullied. We could have justifiably declared our whole home a Superfund site, but the only thing I hate more than poop is paperwork.

Since prior to this incident, I could count on one hand the number of times Tatika had an accident in the house, I do believe she did her best to hold in what she could. As such, I saw no reasons to wag a finger at Tatika more than her own digestive system had already punished her. All we could do was don our hazmat suits and begin the hours of nauseating cleanup to reclaim our residential abode. Even working together, it took most of the night and entire trees' worth of paper towels to mop up the mess, and several more days to air the place out. In the interim, I meditated on two ideas: (1) next year we should do Thanksgiving elsewhere, and (2) perhaps I had underrated the appeal of sleeping in a hammock and should rethink my stance on the matter.

. . .

TATIKA GOING NUMBER TWO IN THE HOUSE STILL ONLY RANKS AS second on our list of largest messes. The reigning bearer of the crud crown is without question Nuk—a superstrong, sleek-coated, bronze-colored gal who finished every race she ever started. Although, one of the years Cole ran the Gin Gin 200, the cryogenic conditions did put her and the entire team to the test.

Cole came prepared, as always, for the worst that winter could dish out. She brought running suits, wind coats, and other protective gear for the dogs to keep them toasty warm. She also packed pounds of pork fat and other high-calorie foods for them to metabolize to help maintain their internal temperatures, since sled dogs process fat the way humans do carbs.

There's no such thing as an easy sled dog race, but this particular event—with an abominable windchill of eighty-five below zero, essentially made for a 200-mile horror corridor for humans and dogs alike. However, as Winston Churchill once said, "When going through hell, don't stop," and over the years we've found this aphorism true for all sled-dog races, even when confronted with temperatures as cold as on the dark side of the moon. Cole and the team persevered and everyone came through the race in good fashion. She not only finished in second place, but received the Humanitarian Award for excellent dog care.

Dogs are like children, though, and when you get them in a big group—such as during a race where huskies from all different parts of Alaska, Canada, and beyond are coming together—they often exchange germs. Over the course of the race Nuk picked up a nasty bug.

"I first noticed something was wrong on the way to the finish," Cole said once back at the truck. "About halfway back, she got diarrhea."

Nuk made it to the finish though, and with the race over, we got a hearty meal of beef, blood broth, and soaked-out kibble into everyone to help them recover, and gave a little extra moisture to Nuk to help prevent her from getting dehydrated.

Cole still had reservations about treating Nuk like the others dogs that were fatigued but otherwise healthy. They were happily getting stowed in the straw-lined cubbyholes of our dog truck to sleep and recover, but Cole felt strongly that Nuk needed more.

"I think she should go in the cab. I think it'd be better for her," Cole said.

I agreed. Since the truck needed to run anyway to stay alive in the frigid temperatures, I figured Nuk would rest better in the softness of one of our down-filled sleeping bags and basking in the heat humming from the vents, while we waited inside the lodge for the other competitors to finish and the closing banquet to begin.

Typically after a race, the dogs are so tired from running, after we feed them their post-race meal, we can let them sleep for stretches of up to six hours before dropping them for a pee and poop break. In terms of holding it, Nuk was usually as constant as a constellation, never having an accident before. Unfortunately, we had mistaken the true nature of her condition. Knowing she was ill, we checked on her after about three hours, but we were already too late.

"It's so . . . creamy?" I said in response to the septic scene that appeared as though someone had loaded half-melted fudge into a shotgun and then sprayed the dash with nothing short of a full-barreled blast.

To say she had experienced irritable bowel syndrome would be as gross an understatement as saying the bomb dropped on Hiroshima was just a little explosion. Nuk's rectum had gone thermonuclear while left unattended. Apparently, not knowing where to go when nature called and not wanting to soil her sleeping-bag bed, she backed up to the dashboard and filed—or perhaps defiled is a more apt description—our vents with defecation.

"Nuk, what did you do girl? What happened in here?" I asked sympathetically while scratching behind her ear, and whether still too sick to muster a defense or feeling too guilty over her incontinence, she never even lifted her head. She remained curled in my sleeping bag, looking up with her big, wet, apologetic eyes, and gave a few soft tail thumps I took to be canine code for "I'm sorry."

We kept several roles of paper towels behind the seat for such occasions, but the problem of cleanup was compounded by the fact that Nuk had not only emptied her bowels more than once, but also because much of the brown slurry had gone into the vents themselves. We physically couldn't get into the heating ducts of the dashboard to wipe out whatever had gone down them.

This left us in a lurch. In the minus forty degree temperatures, following the asphalt trail home for nine hours *without* the heat on was *not* an option, but neither was driving with the windows down unless we wanted to risk being flash frozen. In the end, we had to drive with the heat on and endure the foul fumigation farting out at us the *entire* way.

I wasn't sure we'd survive, and at times we cracked the windows for brief intervals—suffering the stinging iciness that stabbed in to gain a few gulps of fresh air—but somehow we forced ourselves through the long trip. That drive never, before or since, felt as endless as that night, and the only thing that lingered longer than the smell was the memory of the absurd adventure and all we had endured to gain it.

The Great Escape

IT WOULD HAVE BEEN THE GREATEST HALLOWEEN EVER. WE HAD been planning it for months. Cole and I had decided to join my niece and nephew, then five and seven, and their mom, in dressing up for a group theme. Everything was finally fitting into place with the exception of one of our older dogs, Doc, suddenly coming down with an emergency medical condition. Little did I know that night would be one of the longest and most panic-stricken for us and him, and it had little to do with the frightful festivities.

It was a shame, really. Even the weather chose to cooperate for once. Alaska can be a great place to grow up, with one of the few exceptions being the Halloween holiday. Kids usually endure trick-or-treating in a downpour of freezing rain, or worse still, on a foot of snow. Both situations requiring heavy bundling in protective clothing, which means costumes—with fairy wings smashed under down jackets and superhero masks balanced on knit caps—are more flashed at the door than openly enjoyed.

This year, though, temperatures hovered in the upper thirties to lower forties. Leafless branches of tree tips stretched like black cracks up into a sunless, slate-colored sky, while their crinkly brown discards—having long lost their various shades of gold—littered the ground. And it was overcast, but with the rain predicted to hold off, it equated to perfect October weather by Alaskan standards.

Circa the height of the *Harry Potter* film franchise, we had been gathering items for our costumes for some time. My niece and nephew were going as Hermione and Voldemort, respectively, their mom as Professor McGonagall, Cole would don the shroud of a Death Eater, and I somehow ended up being designated to go as the boy wizard himself. I had a Hogwart's-style robe, a scarf in the scarlet-and-gold colors of House Gryffindor, round-lensed glasses, and all week I had practiced to perfection the art of drawing a lightning-shaped scar similar to the one on Harry's forehead.

The only caveat to the candy-gathering fun was earlier that day we had two chores to complete. Drop off one of our dogs, Doc, at the veterinarian for a surgical procedure to remove a sudden and seemingly dangerous golf ball–sized tumor on one of his toes, and, make a whirlwind trip three hours north to Anchorage to pick up a pallet of forty bags of dog food because we were getting low on kibble. Since the entire trip would take us at least seven hours, we had made arrangements for our sister-in-law to pick up Doc from the vet.

We figured there would be no problems because Doc would be woozy from anesthesia, and, we had left *precise* instructions for the doctor and our kin: (a) put Doc in a travel kennel we left there for him to recover in immediately after the surgery; (b) Lift it, with him inside, into the car for the drive to her house; (c) Leave him in the kennel until we got back from the big city.

As usual, despite our best troubleshooting, the situation couldn't have gone worse.

Looking back, it would be easy to point a finger at our sister-in-law for not listening to the acutely detailed guidelines we'd left in our absence. But, to be honest, Doc had made a career of calling up impossible-to-believe feats of strength, and that was exactly what led to the trouble on that ill-fated All Hallow's Eve.

We've known a lot of good dogs over the years, but Doc stood out as a breed apart, and we didn't even get to know him until well past his prime.

He came to us as a retiree from another professional musher attempting to downsize his numbers, primarily older dogs, to keep his kennel at peak performance. Doc still had plenty of life left in him, but at eight years old and going on nine, this was—in dog years—the equivalent of joining the AARP, at least in this musher's eyes, so he decided to move Doc out to focus on his up-and-comers.

Long before he came to our kennel, Doc's rugged masculinity and breathtaking beauty had already caught our attention. He exhibited a unique appearance, the product of recessive genes lining up just so, manifesting in nothing short of a magnificence. His coat was white as freshly fallen snow, not a speck of any other color, and his fur was incredibly thick and dense, like baled straw. His pale pelage further accentuated his piercing blue eyes, as light colored as freshly calved Arctic ice. These gleaming gems became the easiest way to locate him when lying in the yard where he freely roamed. We'd scan the snow till we detected two sapphires staring back at us, and when that failed—often when he slept—we'd scout for his bright pink nose.

All huskies have an inherent zest for running and pulling, but with Doc it seemed like much more than that. I'm not sure if he felt the rush of biological chemicals like those that give human joggers their "runner's high," or perhaps more of a metaphysical euphoria closer to the Zen-like state achieved by meditating Buddhist monks. All I know for certain is when in harness and out on the trail—no matter whether trotting, pacing, or loping—he wasn't just completely at ease. He was actually at peace, as if in more of a zone, a deep rhythmic zone. Because of this hallmark, he thoroughly seemed born to run.

And with a weight of roughly seventy pounds, when Doc dug his paws in, there wasn't much he couldn't power his way through. Because of this proclivity, Doc had seen a lot of racing in his prime with his previous musher and others he frequently found himself lent and leased to. Doc had done just about every mid-distance race in the state, and proved a valuable member of a championship team in the 1,000-mile Yukon Quest.

After moving to our kennel and with still a bit of gas in his tank, Cole's first race with Doc was the Tustumena 100, and once again his

Doc, whom we took in as a retiree, proved he still had plenty of life and pulling power in him, as we witnessed during a Halloween that was frightful to him and us.

contributions helped her secure victory. Not long after that, Doc's purpose shifted from being part of a winning team to training our younger dogs for future victories. Doc's brutish strength, complemented by a sweet disposition toward people and other dogs, made him a natural fit for serving as a role model for the puppy team. His seasoned leadership skills bestowed unsurpassed talent upon many of our dogs that eventually became main racers. By running next to Doc when they were pups, these understudies learned to run in front of a long string of dogs, and hold the team out in stressful situations.

Doc's forte for heeding the command of "line out" ranked among the best of any dog to ever hold the title of leader. This term instructs the lead dogs to stretch the gangline out, so that—during hooking up dogs, taking breaks on the trail, or putting them away after a run—no slack gets produced to tangle anyone up. Less-disciplined lead dogs, when the team stops, will widely wander side to side, or, in the worst scenario, frantically buttonhook around and run back to visit with the musher or check the sled bag for snacks. These latter leaders can create gangline tangles dangerous enough to snap a furry limb, or worse, if looped around the neck, strangle a dog.

Not Doc though. Once Doc lined out, he stood statuesque, and it didn't matter how many young and wild dogs were behind him pulling in a tug-of-war or diving to the sides of the trail. He never failed at this command. He held his ground like a rock monolith, never budging, never wavering.

After seeing how well he did training our first batch of dogs acquired from various mushers and animal shelters, and since we were still building the numbers of our kennel, we decided to breed Doc in the hopes of producing more dogs like him. Like the Seven Dwarfs–themed litter he was a part of (hence his name), Doc also sired seven pups, and many of these dogs got their daddy's traits. Two dogs in that litter, Yeti, a forty-pound, calico-colored female, and Waylon, an eighty-pound male, big like his pop but with a panther-black coat, were only a year old when they ran with Cole in the 200-mile Chatanika Challenge, an arduous race they won together. From that day forward, every race our kennel has competed in had at least one or more of Doc's pups on the team and like their father, they never faltered.

As the years passed and Doc grew older with us, he ran less and less, until he finally stopped running in the team altogether. We tried to retire him into the house, like we do with most of our geriatric dogs, but Doc seemed to endure more than enjoy his time indoors. He was content to stay out in the yard, wandering the perimeter to weave through the swaying fireweed blossoms of summer, and sniffing out snowshoe hares living under old stumps and piles of decaying deadfall in winter.

He eventually quit using his own doghouse and instead took up napping in the various abodes of dogs in the kennel who he cottoned to, or peacefully resided under a table set up in the yard where we cut fish daily to hand out for breakfast. We began spreading straw under it once we realized his preference, and served him his dinner there too. Still, he enjoyed sneaking off briefly to steal a bone or chew toy from another husky who had haphazardly made the mistake of falling asleep with their prized possession unsecured in their own doghouses. He also gathered any gloves, boots, or other clothing we left on our deck to dry, caching them with his other items.

Still, no matter how much treasure he tucked away, he would always leave his enclave to greet us with tail-wagging excitement as we stepped from the car after a long day at work, or to accompany us on short walks as we left the cabin in the evening to use the outhouse. Because of this intimate relationship with Doc, we took immediate notice when he showed up one day with a limp.

Examining him, the middle toe of his back foot appeared swollen, and we tracked its increase in size with each passing day, our concern correlating to its growth. Fearing cancer—a scourge of older animals—we made an appointment to have the toe looked at by a veterinarian. After a few X-rays, the doctor gave the prognosis that the toe should come off. Their first open appointment for surgery: Halloween day.

Apparently the surgery went well. Doc lost the digit, got a few stitches, and had his foot carefully wrapped in a protective bandage. The doctor also sent him home with a little extra sedative in his system, to keep him calm since it was imperative he not bear any weight on the paw for the first few days.

As per our instructions, the veterinarian recovered Doc from his anesthesia in the kennel we had left and helped load him into the back-hatch of our sister-in-law's Subaru. She drove him to her house, roughly five minutes away in Kenai, where Cole and I were supposed to pick him up a couple hours later, and that's when and where the situation took a turn for the worse.

Rather than leaving him in his half-sleep state in the kennel in the car, she decided to bring him in the house. This would have been a benevolent deed had she only closed her garage door after she pulled in, but before attempting to roust Doc out. Instead, she pulled into the garage, went to the back and unloaded Doc, and with a seemingly secure grip on his collar, she pressed the remote for the garage door.

The thunderous clanking of metal, the startling slap of chains, and the grinding vibrations of the rollers could easily enough scare any dog on a good day, and Doc was far from his best at that moment. Living most of his life in kennels in remote wooded areas, he wasn't used to the mechanical sounds of more modern suburban life. This, combined with his half-coherent post-surgery state, well, simply put, the sounds of the garage door scraping closed scared the bejeezus right out of poor old Doc.

He did what he knew best. He began to run, pulling our sister-in-law right along with him. She clung to his collar for all she was worth, but he pulled her along, first on her feet for a few yards, then overpowering her and dragging her, rag doll style, next to him for several more yards. Sustaining scraped elbows and knees, she finally released her grip out of fear for her own well-being, and Doc dashed off.

"I just didn't realize how powerful he was," she admitted later. She had two dogs of her own, including a husky mix, but in terms of their power, pet dogs and in particular lifelong sled dogs, are as different from each other as a bicycle is to a motorcycle. An unforgettable lesson she had learned the hard way.

She set off after Doc, but her house was near a large, undeveloped swath of forest that within just a few miles opened up into an even larger wooded area, part of the 1.92-million-acre Kenai National Wildlife Refuge. If Doc were to roam into the refuge, he could get so lost in the vast wilderness that we'd never be able to locate him, or worse still, a hungry bear or pack of wolves would hone in on the smell of his still-bleeding stump and make a meal of him.

Gruesome as these notions were, these were the first two thoughts that went through my mind when we arrived just before dark and heard what happened from our sister-in-law. She had burst from the house and through eyes welling with tears and a storm of sincere apologies told us her tale of the great escape. I felt like I had stopped breathing entirely when I heard the bad news.

Knowing Doc wandered in unfamiliar territory, far from the trails he knew and that could lead him home, we acted immediately. Darkness would soon be falling and we knew with it would come hordes of trick-or-treaters clogging the streets. Not only could they hamper our search efforts, but the very nature of the unconventional appearance of the costume-clad—combined with the shouts and shrieks of these children riding a euphoric state of sugar-fueled ecstasy—would be enough to further drive Doc away from civilization.

Back then, our niece and nephew were too young to understand the gravity of the situation, and so it was decided they shouldn't be deprived of enjoying the evening. They went trick-or-treating with their mom, while we sprinted to the last place Doc was seen. We looked down in the small ravine, detritus dank and densely packed with spruce and a few leafless deciduous trees looking forlorn and bleak as our prospects. I called out Doc's name and heard nothing but the echo of my own voice. The silence felt like weight. We hiked a few hundred yards in both directions while continuing to shout his name, but there was no sign of him. Our hearts sank like the setting sun.

We drove to the closest hardware store and purchased two heavy-duty, oil-can sized flashlights that ran on the big twelve-volt batteries. By the time we returned, the neighborhood was heavily congested with honking cars dropping off kids, and the cul-de-sacs were crowded with vampires, ninja turtles, witches, and other weirdos. Many were waving their own flashlights and fluorescent glow sticks, all giggling and screaming to each other in excited high-pitched voices. The costume-crazed ran from house to house, in front of each one a flickering orange glow emanating from carved jack-o-lanterns.

Nothing short of a rural dog's worst nightmare.

We refused to give up though. We waded through the children, going street to street hollering Doc's name, but unfortunately a few wisenheimers, not understanding the urgency of our situation, began echoing "Doc" back to us from near and far. We decided to return to the woods and continue our search there, but many hours later—cold, hungry, and covered in bramble scratches and mosquito bites—we were no closer to finding him. At one point we even got harassed by the police after someone saw our flashlight beams in the woods and mistook us for pranksters up to no good.

The whole evening disheartened us and as the darkness of night finally began to give way to the cobalt blue of a nearing dawn, we felt heavily fatigued and emotionally drained. Beginning to lose faith, we made a couple of early morning calls. I contacted a local flightseeing operation, explained our situation, and made plans to charter a small plane. My thought being, since it was late fall and most trees had dropped their leaves, from the air an all-white Doc would stand out among all the brown and green below. The pilot said he would need a few hours to fuel up and make other arrangements to accommodate this late-season plea.

Cole, on the other hand, called a musher friend of ours, the person from whom we'd adopted Doc. We thought since he and his wife had known him longer than we had, maybe they'd have some idea for getting him back. As it turned out, his wife not only had a trick up her sleeve, but was also willing to help us try it out.

She explained that while waiting at numerous trailheads and finish lines for her husband and the team to come in, she always left the dog truck running, not only to keep herself warm, but also because she believed the low rumbling of the diesel engine would give the dogs a sound they could recognize, to know they were getting close to the end of the run.

While Cole and I were away at a copy store making 1,000 "Lost Dog" fliers with Doc's picture on them and the details of his disappearance, we told our friend the last location Doc had been spotted and she agreed to go there in their dog truck.

Pavlov would have been proud.

Our friend wasn't there idling for more than a few minutes before she saw Doc limp his way out of the woods. She called immediately with the good news, and we arranged to meet her at the veterinarian's office, since she said Doc needed medical attention.

When we got there, we realized she hadn't undersold his condition. Doc's paw looked ghastly. It was grotesquely swollen, his bandage and stitches were long gone, and as evident from the debris in his open wound, he had run through the mud and leaf litter all night with the laceration exposed. The doctor also determined he suffered from dehydration, likely a combination of shock from the traumatic nature of the night, and not having food or water in more than thirty-six hours, as he had been fasted before his operation.

Doc went back into surgery and got re-stitched up and re-bandaged with a clean dressing. This time he was released to *our* care and we got him home as quickly as we could for some much needed rest and recuperation for all of us. The three of us slept like bears in a winter den. Looking back, I may have missed out on pretending to be Harry Potter for the night, but our misadventure was one comparable to anything the young wizard ever faced, and, for me, that evening will forever be known as the "Night-That-Shall-Not-Be-Named."

A Maternal Metoo

THE FIRST PINK AND GOLD RAYS OF THE DAY PEAKED THROUGH my kitchen curtains as I savored the taste of a steaming mug of coffee. Beside me sat my pajama-clad daughter, Lynx, in her highchair and contently cooing to herself at the delight of picking up a Cheerio and putting it in her mouth, a recently learned skill she had not yet mastered. As such, Metoo, our part-time lead dog and full-time house dog, patiently lounged beneath Lynx to catch any of the little whole-grain Os that clumsy fingers might fumble to the floor.

Clamping my warm cup of joe with one hand, my other held the morning paper and as I scanned the classifieds an ad caught my eye. It was one, the likes of which, I have seen countless times before and since. The bold print words read: "Loving dog. Free to good home. Having baby and can't keep him."

Due mostly to the Rockwellian-picturesque tranquillity between canine and child that surrounds me, I find the idea of someone planting a family pet with a new owner—simply because of impending parenthood— a grotesquely misguided notion, and one that demonstrates a way of thinking as black and white as the advertisement itself.

From birth, Lynx came home to eight house dogs of varying sizes and temperaments, as well as forty more huskies living in the front yard.

However, long before Lynx ever set one of her little pink feet in our house, Metoo sensed, or perhaps more likely smelled, something different about Colleen starting around the end of her first trimester.

I've always been curious about this ability in dogs. I've read enough books to know that the average dog can smell hundreds of times better than us short-schnozzed humans, but I wonder what do the perfumed particles their super sniffers isolate actually smell like?

Is the subtle scent of explosives to a bomb-detecting dog as acrid as burning hair? Does an internal disease like cancer waft with the sulfurous stench of rotten eggs? For dogs that can distinguish drugs, is the first olfactory sensation similar to having a hive of bees buzzing in their snout?

If so, then I envision the aroma of new life growing in the womb could only be the exact opposite, perhaps as sweet as the smell of hot cinnamon buns baking in the oven. That's how it seemed for Metoo, who acted like a kid staking out a choice spot in the kitchen to wait for a sweet confection to finish baking. She constantly postured and positioned to get close to Cole's growing baby bump, and hardly a night of her pregnancy went by without Metoo's head resting on her belly.

Metoo came into our lives as a result of providing a temporary home for a close friend's very pregnant sled dog, which had accidentally been bred while running the Iditarod. It's common for females to go into their spring heat cycle during the race, and while mushers are grabbing a few winks in a checkpoint, dogs will occasionally find the energy for a roll in the hay, rather than sleeping on it as they should.

This canine harlot's owner was a commercial fisherman who would be at the height of the salmon-catching season and out at sea when the dog was due. We consented to take on the responsibility for our friend, and a few weeks later, we came home from work to find six wiggling and whimpering little neonates nursing from their mama.

They grew quickly, too quickly, like all puppies do in the eyes of their owners. It wasn't long until they were seven weeks old and in need of their first vaccinations. Most dogs get their first booster at this time because it is when the natural immunity-providing colostrum of their

Metoo, a couple of weeks after overcoming her near-deadly illness. Although she was still skinny, she was otherwise spunky and ready to follow us everywhere.

mother's milk begins to taper off. What's tricky is that the amount of immunity they got from their mom is highly variable. If a vaccine is given too soon, the antibodies in their mother's milk will block the effectiveness of a vaccine, but if a vaccine isn't given soon enough after the natural immunities have begun to fade, the pups could be susceptible to any number of diseases.

Living in a neighborhood dense with other kennels within a few square miles of our home, dog germs are spread throughout the environment as thickly as mosquitoes after the spring hatch. Despite our best efforts, within weeks of the first vaccine, three little ones in the litter appeared to have contracted the plague of the puppy world. The feisty youngsters we had grown to love, and that days before seemed endlessly energetic, abruptly became limp and lifeless. They had little to no appetite, and anything consumed didn't stay down long. It either was vomited up or came out as diarrhea with the distinct coppery, rotten-blood smell of parvo.

Metoo suffered the worst from the virulent catastrophe. She looked as though the grim reaper already had her by the scruff. We rushed her and the other two infected puppies to the veterinary clinic, and were more appalled than shocked to be turned away at the first facility.

"I'm sorry, we'd rather you not bring them in the building," said a flinty eyed technician.

Incensed, we demanded to speak to a veterinarian directly, who quickly came out with a just-took-a-deep-breath look. He continued the shooing-us-out effort, citing the high contagiousness of the virus combined with his belief that most creatures that contracted it weren't going to pull through anyway. It's tough to articulate the depth of the helpless feelings that welled within me from wanting and being willing to help these poor puppies, and having those with methods and means turn a blind eye to their plight.

Dejected, but determined to not give up on the pups, we took our businesses elsewhere. We sped off to a second clinic that took us in. They let us know there was not a high likelihood of survivability, but agreed to do what they could to help. Following their diagnosis that confirmed the obvious, they sent us home with several bags of IV fluids, injectable antibiotics, and antinausea and antidiarrheal medications.

Over the course of the next week, Cole and I barely slept and took turns calling in sick to work due to the twenty-four-hour care we provided to the pups. Triage became our sole function in life. Whenever one pup slept, another got fluids, since it took two people: one to hold it still, and the other person to monitor the injection site and watch the flow rate. As fast as these life-saving liquids went into one pup, foul-smelling stool projectile-squirted from the rear end of one of the other patients. Had we invested stock in the paper towel industry before this fiasco we could have been very rich people.

After ten days, slowly—very slowly—all the puppies began coming back to life, nibbling and keeping down small amounts of easily digestible foods like cottage cheese, or boiled chicken and rice. Metoo was the only one not interested in food, which was worrisome in itself, but also since she was merely seven weeks old when she contracted the virus. This meant she didn't have a lot of fat to begin with, and while fighting the canine flu she basically survived by burning up her small body's reserves.

"This one has me very nervous," I told Cole, while cradling the pup to my chest, where she lived for warmth as well as nurturing affection, day and night, for the better part of the two weeks prior. "I'm afraid she may survive the parvo, but succumb to starvation."

People throw around the cliché "skin and bones" often, but in Metoo's case, there really wasn't a more apt description for how much she had dwindled physically. Lifting her felt like picking up a small bag filled with sticks. She had a positive mental attitude, but her movements were poor and rickety. Just going out for walks or wagging her tail at the sight of one of us coming in the room appeared to exhaust her.

Despite the obvious fatigue she felt from even the simplest physical tasks, when not in our arms, she had become inseparable from us during the course of her treatment. Weak and winded, she mustered the strength to follow us around our cabin turned trauma ward, and never left our heels when we carried her outside and set her down for bathroom breaks. She insisted on being everywhere with us as though constantly saying "Me too, me too," so we finally settled on that for her formal appellation.

Eventually Metoo's appetite increased and she made a full recovery, and while we never held our breath that she could completely overcome setbacks from her early life ailments and transform into a full-fledged sled dog, as she got older she continued to express her same dogged determination to be with us. For weeks, she ran along with teams we were conditioning and suffered no latent effects, so one day we put her in harness and plugged her into a string. In terms of fitness and performance, she looked indistinguishable from any other dog.

She continued to train and eventually displayed an aptitude for the lead and swing positions, making valuable contributions to our race teams over the years. She expressed more than a zest for running, her elation at hookup being closer to sheer ecstasy. She had an unusual habit of pronk-ing—bounding off the ground simultaneously on all fours—more than rearing up or hammering forward in harness while waiting for a run to begin. As a result, she appears to be levitating in nearly every photograph of her taken in race starting chutes.

Due to her still unabated attachment issues, she *had* to be on the team whenever we ran, and particularly when we raced. We found this out the hard way during Cole's second Iditarod, which Metoo was slated to be part of.

On one of the final training runs in February, Metoo took a bad step and broke a toe. This dinged digit eliminated her as one of the sixteen candidates attempting to take on 1,000 miles of Alaskan mountain ranges, frozen rivers, and winding timber trails, an endeavor that requires each dog to be 100 percent healthy.

Since she also lived the life of a house dog, we always took her along with us in the car or dog truck, wherever we went. She had grown pretty used to the idea of riding in the cab and lounging until we got somewhere, so we decided she should ride along with us to the start of the Iditarod, to keep me company on the nearly four-hour drive home after Cole left the starting chute. Thinking only how this arrangement would comfort her, we hadn't considered how she would react when she realized the team was heading down the trail and she was not with them.

She did not take the news well.

At the sign of the first harness coming out, she erupted in a hysterical conniption in the cab. We had left the windows cracked just enough to prevent her from climbing out, and she used this inch-wide gap to let her dissatisfaction be known. She slid her head sideways through the opening, while emitting a high-pitched, yet utterly mournful howl, repeatedly. When that didn't get our attention, she began scratching at the window feverishly in an attempt to dig her way out of the door.

Cole and I were focused on getting the team out of the starting chute, so we had to ignore Metoo's full-throttle tantrum until the task at hand was completed. By the time Cole finally departed for Nome, going out in her randomly drawn starting position of forty-second, Metoo had completely exhausted herself from her Category 5 cyclone in the cab. The interior of the windows was entirely fogged over and sweating with rivulets of condensation from the heat Metoo had generated while going wild. She had ripped stuffing from the seats, chewed the seat belt straps to pieces, and gnawed the buckles into useless clumps of jagged plastic.

What she had suffered was more a clinical bout of separation hyper-activity than separation anxiety, and with one of us finally back in the cab, Metoo—completely spent—passed out with her head in my lap, barely moving the entire drive home.

Knowing her fervent attachment to us, as Cole's due date drew near, we looked forward with excitement—yet felt some trepidation—to how Metoo would be with our newborn. Our fears were compounded when Lynx's birth did not go as planned.

As our rugged lifestyle of being Alaskan mushers may indicate, we're not fans of American materialism or its corresponding consumer-driven lifestyle, and our Luddite tendencies extend to avoiding the money-making business of modern medicine. We decided Lynx wouldn't be born in a place where birth was looked at as a medical predicament rather than a natural occurrence.

Alternately we considered a home birth, but after weighing the factors that we lived twenty-five miles from the nearest hospital, Lynx was due during breakup (when vehicles are wont to get stuck in the mud), and that delivering an infant in a home with eight shedding, less-than-civilized dogs would be insane, we decided to use a midwife and plan for Lynx to be born at a natural-birth center in town, less than a quarter mile from the hospital should an emergency occur.

Cole's pregnancy went great and an ever-vigilant Metoo was never far from her side. As the final days drew near, Cole's water broke right on time (and luckily, *after* a full day of dog chores). We called the midwife and told her we were on our way in. Metoo came with.

The midwife met us at the birth center in the wee hours of a Monday morning. She had drawn a warm bath in the birth tub for Cole to soak in while her contractions grew more intense and closer together. I did what I could to lend emotional support, taking occasional breaks checking on Metoo to calm my nerves.

After several hours, and following one last powerful push, my small, scrunched-up daughter shot out like a fresh team bursting from a starting chute. Being a new father, and not expecting her to enter the world with quite so much velocity, I nearly fumbled my slippery newborn. I cut the umbilical cord, and then we beamed at our creation, becoming sappy from the immediate and intoxicating effects of parental love and the absurd amount of fear that comes with bringing a precious new life into the world. Metoo howled from outside, possibly in protest of her isolation, but I like to think it was because she sensed our pack had grown by one.

Then complications arose. As Cole passed the placenta, it tore, creating a potentially dangerous situation since she would bleed continually till it came completely out. In Alaska, midwives are legally very limited as to which medical procedures they are allowed to do. With only one option, the midwife, in her most soothing voice, said, "Now, don't panic, but we're going to have to head over to the hospital." She then calmly called the emergency room and explained Cole's condition so they could prepare for her arrival, while I anxiously awaited the two minutes—which felt more like two millennia—until the ambulance arrived.

Going the midwife route, we had already heard nine months of poo-pooing from people whose only idea of a midwife was the antiquated image of a prune-faced old woman, dressed in traditional Quaker clothes, bringing in steaming towels as the sole medical preparation for the impending birth. However, it was a decision made with months of prior research, and one we were—and still are—confident was right for us.

In that moment, though, when the two EMTs entered the birth center, I'm sure their survey of the scene brought to mind something other than a well-thought-out decision. I immediately wondered if they mistook us for devout Grateful Dead followers or some other hippie-types. This I attribute to three kooky coincidences: (1) Lacking a night's sleep due to Cole's labor and the stress of that ordeal, I looked completely stoned, from my bloodshot eyes to my mouth hinged open; (2) When Cole's water broke, the first thing I grabbed to clothe myself while running out of the house was a brilliantly technicolored tie-dyed shirt with so much bright, swirling magnificence, it made anyone who looked at it too long feel like they were stoned; (3) On my lower extremities I was solely, and equally inappropriately, wearing swimming trunks and completely barefoot from having been only moments before in the birthing pool to massage Cole during labor.

I'm certain the only way this scene could have appeared like full *Reefer Madness* to the EMTs was if I had been shouting "Dave's not here, man!" while clutching a glass bong in my hand, but in reality, I held the miniscule Lynx—swaddled in a bathroom towel—so they could immediately attend to my wife.

Cole laid face-up and naked in a crimson puddle from where she was quickly bleeding out. The midwife was kneeling at the foot of the bed holding a ceramic bowl with the portion of placenta Cole had passed. The EMTs assessed the situation and said to no one in particular, "We need to get her onto the gurney to get her into the ambulance." They seemed uncertain where to grab Cole though, since she was completely nude, spread-eagle, and still partially attached to the pasta bowl full of placenta.

Never one to dodge hard work even when compromised, Cole volunteered "I can just climb onto the board," and proceeded to prop herself up on her feet and elbows, in a bit of a stomach-high arch, and crab walked onto the gurney.

The EMTs buckled Cole down and loaded her into the ambulance, followed first by the midwife who kept stride with the blood-filled bowl tethering her to Cole, and then by me, with Lynx still in my arms. I didn't look over at our parked car, but could hear Metoo wailing wildly in the distance.

The ride to the hospital was a quick jaunt, so the EMTs made the decision not to start an IV—their first mistake. They also opted to take her directly to the maternity ward, rather than the emergency room, which would also come back to bite us in the ass.

The only pediatric doctor on duty (who coincidentally was also the town mayor and an Iditarod veteran himself) was in the middle of performing a C-section, yet after about twenty minutes, he came in briefly to assess the situation. He immediately, manually, and rather abruptly—to Cole's wide-eyed surprise and discomfort—retrieved the retained placenta with his gloved hand.

He then told the two nurses present to start an IV. This would help with the blood loss and allow them to give, through the IV, an injection that would cause her uterus to contract and hopefully slow or stop the bleeding. He said this would give him time to finish the other procedure, and he'd be back as soon as he could.

The two nurses looked at each other like they hoped the other would volunteer to start the IV, and reluctantly one finally did. The reason for their hesitation quickly became apparent. As the nurse attempted to find a vein in Cole's arm, her hand shook like she had Parkinson's, and she—astonishingly—verbalized her discomfort with the task.

"I don't know why the EMTs didn't do this," she complained. "They're so much better at it."

The nurse tried and failed several times in one of Cole's arms before giving up and asking the other nurse to—pun intended—take a stab at Cole's other limb. This second nurse had as much success, or lack thereof, and between the two of them, they nearly ruined the veins in Cole's arms for any chance of an IV that day.

During the time they flunked at this medical procedure that seemed like it should be 101 material in nursing school, Cole continued to bleed out in a conspicuous way. She had saturated her sheets and mattress, and a large red sea began forming under her hospital bed.

Worse still, she grew less and less coherent with each passing hour and her skin color turned pallid and developed an almost waxy appearance. Still, somehow, this fact only seemed alarming to our midwife and me, who were helpless to do anything but wring our hands.

Every fear we had had that led us to not choose a hospital for Lynx's birth was now coming horribly true.

Finally, after more than two hours, the doctor came back in and from the vexed look on his face, it was clear he too gauged the severity of the situation. He immediately chided the nurses for their ineptitude and within seconds had an IV in Cole's arm and flowing. Surmising that Cole teetered on the brink of bleeding to death, he told them to immediately strip everything she had bled on and weigh it, then weigh the same items from a clean-linen closet. This was to assess the volume of blood

Metoo, one of our exceptionally skilled lead dogs, showing she was equally devoted to being a family dog. She vigorously protected our newborn daughter from the moment she arrived home with a vigilance that reached near-obsessive proportions.

lost, which turned out to be more than 50 percent of the blood in her body.

He even mentioned the possibility of a transfusion, but ultimately decided against it. Eventually Cole stabilized, but the huge loss of blood meant she couldn't stand for days. She didn't have the blood pressure for it, and would immediately become light-headed or faint if she stood for longer than a few seconds. The lack of blood also greatly compromised her ability to recover from childbirth itself, so even though she had exercised and worked in the dog yard until the day Lynx was born, she spent weeks afterward bedridden at home.

It was during this time that Metoo's true colors really shined through. While we had always thought of her as being inseparable from us, her vigilance with Lynx became downright obsessive from the first second we came home. Upon arrival from the hospital, Metoo crammed her nose into the vicinity of Cole's privates, sniffed, then sniffed at Lynx's tiny head. Her eyes sparkled as she made the connection, that one came from the other.

From then on, during Cole's entire recovery Metoo lay with her head on Cole's belly nearly twenty-four hours a day, the only exceptions being when I would prod Metoo outside to relive herself or into the kitchen to begrudgingly scarf down a quick meal. And when she was resting on Cole, she *always* did so in a way that she could watch where the baby was.

I seemed to be included in the circle of two people who could hold Lynx, but if anyone else approached—human or canine—she would cast a stare as stern as an alpha wolf's and bare her teeth while making a deep, guttural growl, like the low rumbling of not-so-distant thunder. This persisted for months, which made it a little dicey when family or friends came by to get a gander at our new addition, but we also found it endearing that Metoo took her self-assigned role as watchful protector so seriously.

Despite all the pre-birth fears we had about juggling our time between our dual roles of new parents and full-time devoted dog owners, the transition to having our own new pup was remarkably smooth, I think partially from so many years of our lives filled with animals. Perceptive at decoding the body language, slight signals, and subtle nuances of non-speaking creatures, we parlayed this skill to parenthood without even realizing it.

Lynx made it easy, too, by not being a fussy baby, and like her mom, being athletic from the start. As soon as she could hold her head up, we began wearing her in a front-facing sling so she could take in all the sights, sounds, and smells of the dog yard. We took her on short dog runs on the four-wheeler in fall, and then the sled in winter. Bundled up in layers of snowsuits that made her look like a miniature Stay Puft Marshmallow Man, she always smiled and giggled from the sled as the dogs galloped out of the yard, but inevitably the rhythmic movements would lull her to sleep before we returned home.

Metoo lead the team for Lynx's first dog run and many thereafter. In the house they became best buds. Lynx was happy to get a wet-nosed greeting from any dog, but as soon as she could crawl, she would seek out Metoo to feel the tickle of her whiskers, to lift her lips to get a glimpse at those white things underneath that she didn't have yet, and sometimes

When our daughter, Lynx, was born, she and Metoo bonded immediately. With mixed emotions, we also realized Metoo was sharing in the child-rearing duties. She taught Lynx many tricks of the trade to being a sled dog, including howling with the pack.

simply to snuggle onto Metoo when she needed some rest. It was a magnetic fascination from the start.

Perhaps from being raised by us as much as her own mom, Metoo cared for Lynx like she was her own pup. She always made sure the other dogs weren't being too rough with Lynx, and never disciplined her or showed any aggression, even when Lynx would tug an ear, dangle from her tail, or discomfort her in some other manner. She would just gently paw at her to quit, which Lynx did, usually by her choice, but occasionally by ours.

As Lynx's size and coordination grew, so too did their bond. Outside they'd cavort, playing their own version of hide-and-seek with Lynx running to a place she thought concealed her cleverly. Metoo would find her, play bowing, bucking wildly into the air, and her tail perpetually wagging once she had ferreted Lynx out. As Lynx grew older still, she figured out throwing a stick meant Metoo would diligently retrieve it, and for weeks fetch became more Lynx's favorite pastime than Metoo's.

My daughter seemed to see everything in her world through a lens of dog culture, much of it learned from her daily and personal interactions with Metoo. Cole's hair flows to past her knees, and when she French braided it, Lynx would say, "Mommy has her tail on." When I used the chain saw, she would tell me it "barks loud." Being raised in the woods, when we made shopping forays in town, she described the speeding cars as "running by too fast." And for months, Lynx called her hands her hands, but referred to her lower extremities as her "hind feet."

With mixed emotions, we even realized Metoo had taught Lynx how to howl, as all the dogs do after mealtime and at dusk. Together they would sit on the couch, their noses pointed to the ceiling, crooning at the top of their lunges, and each loving every minute of the shared song. Lynx learned the language of the pack—her pack, the one she was born into— and she learned it long before she acquired the language of her own kind.

This is the reason why ads that read "Dog: Free to good home, having a baby and can't keep it," really chap my ass. While so many people are quick to get rid of man's best friend, we didn't and wouldn't give up on a canine member just because we were adding a new, tiny human to the family, and because of that decision, Lynx has had a furry childhood friend and unwavering protector ever since.

Not Office Material

A T THE TIME I PENNED THIS BOOK, I WAS EARNING MY LIVING BY working from home, partially to raise my daughter, Lynx, and mostly because no one would have me. It's the truth; I don't deny it, primarily because the situation had nothing to do with my work ethic or skill as a writer. Rather, the remand to my domestic domicile had everything to do with the hopeless impossibility of maintaining even a modicum of office decorum as a man cohabiting with forty dogs.

I know self-imposed isolation may not be the cure for everyone, and certainly isn't the case for those fancy-pants operations relying on handlers to do the lion's share of the dirty work, but since Cole and I had almost exclusively been a mom-and-pop operation with our dogs, it meant we did *all* the training, feeding, poop scooping, etc. Also, unlike many folks, we had at least eight permanent house dogs living with us (and one cat), and tried to rotate through the dogs from the yard, bringing in a different one each night to indulge them with some couch time or shared space in our bed.

The pocket-sized sixteen-foot-by-sixteen-foot cabin we lived in had no running water, and lacked cupboards, counters, and most importantly, closets for most of our mushing years. This lack of lock-away spaces meant scarcely any item of clothing in our tiny home, no matter how clean, escaped being thickly overlaid with dog fur. Some days my garments appeared so woolen, I think some suspected I favored a wardrobe entirely made up of mohair sweaters and matching pants.

Adding to our dilemma, with the exception of one matchbook-sized mirror I used once a week to shave, our tiny cabin was devoid of any reflective objects. Don't ask why. I really have no answer, other than my wife and I clearly exhibit no interest or dignity regarding our own appearance or that of our partner.

Seriously though, if pressed for an explanation, I would probably attribute our lack of mirrors to our lives prior to being in the cabin. Before we moved to Alaska, we had lived in the woods for six months while hiking the 2,168-mile Appalachian Trail. Over that introspective time—away from cell phones, fancy-schmancy overpriced lattes, and the superficialities that dominate mainstream society as a whole—we learned what values were essential in our daily lives and, as odd as it sounds, seeing ourselves was not that important. As we integrated back into the civilized world, somehow we never changed this opinion of not needing a mirror.

For soon-to-be obvious reasons, this absence of reflective items represented a huge oversight on our parts. Working in an office and dealing with customers, clients, and what have you, a person needs to have at least a mild awareness of their appearance, for others, if not for their own self. I know that . . . *now*.

I learned of my folly the hardest way possible, while working in Kenai—a city of about 7,000—that at roughly thirty miles away, is the closest town to us. First settled by Natives around 1,000 BC, in more recent times Kenai's become increasingly populated by those looking to take advantage of the area's resources, starting with Russian fur traders in the mid-1700s, followed by gold miners in the 1800s, and commercial fishermen and homesteaders in the 1900s. Nowadays it's primarily those working in the fields of gas and oil exploration—or exploitation, depending on your world view—that make up the populace, and these folks read the newspaper, which was where I found employment.

During this period, Cole and I adhered to an exhaustingly rigorous dog-training schedule. Working full-time, we would wake at 6:00 A.M. and

Yeti, Rolo, Colleen, Lynx, me, and Metoo at the end of a snowy night run.
Most of our training with the dogs took place in the dark, after work,
until I switched to writing from home.

feed all the dogs their soaked-out kibble and meat-gruel mixture, gulp back a cup of coffee, and then begin making the long dark drive to work. Between the icy roads, and dodging moose that incessantly walked on or across them, the commute often took us close to an hour. We'd then work eight hours at our respective jobs, drive home again in the dark (since at this time of year the sun was only up from about 10:00 A.M. to 4:00 P.M.), then change into our mushing gear, hook up two dog teams, mush for five to six hours, put all dogs and gear away, then feed and clean the dog yard again. Afterward, we fed ourselves, around 2:00 A.M. and would finally go to bed to get what perpetually seemed like just enough sleep to stay alive, but not really enough to function on all cylinders.

With such a hectic schedule, we prearranged as much as possible to shave seconds anywhere we could, and one of my routines before going to bed included laying out clothes for work the next day. Honestly, if I could have slept in them I would have. It always seemed to work well enough for my parents when I was a kid and they had to get me up at the crack of dawn to drive somewhere.

My work clothes looked shabby enough though, without me showing up in garb heavily wrinkled from a brief night's sleep in them. I already stood out by being one of the only people in the office who didn't wear a tie. I've always had a wild heart I guess, and ties—particularly in the workplace—were to me the symbolic embodiment of a noose, or a leash at the very least. Either way I never wanted one around my neck, then or now.

On the eve of my education about needing a mirror, I carried out my usual pre-bedtime ritual. Over a chair, I laid out a pair of khaki pants and a Navy blue sweater, then slid under the sheets hoping to put an end to my sleep-deprived stupor. Instead, a fitful few hours of tossing and turning were as close to sleep as I got.

The problem on this occasion wasn't due to a dog, but our cat. He seemed to be trying to best some personal record for how many hair balls he could consecutively wretch up, so several times an hour he would emit an awful, unceremonious sound.

Wearily I awoke the next morning, did all my usual chores, then pulled on my office civvies, and drove to work with Cole. She affectionately pointed out that, as usual, my lower eyelids sagged exposing the red rims around my irises, but otherwise I looked "good enough" for another day in the office. To be fair, the place I worked was like a tableau of living people carrying out perfunctory tasks. The place was so lifeless, it seemed as if somehow the watercooler had been spiked with Xanax. Short of streaking, emitting a leg-liftingly loud fart, or bringing in a communal baked good that wasn't gluten free, not much would have gotten my coworkers to raise an eyebrow anyway.

Our office was one large, faux-wood paneled room, flickering fluorescent lights above, and tacky well-worn '70s carpet below a half-dozen desks with computer monitors and keyboards. Most days the air wafted with the scent of rotten mushrooms or expensive cheese depending on your palate for these kinds of things. No barriers or cubicles separated me from the other journalists and lay-out minions.

I took my position at my own desk that morning, placed a few calls, and typed a story. I, as always, tried my best to drum up small talk with my fellow employees, as well as any living creature who entered the office from another part of the building for any reason, so long as it frittered away a few minutes of the mind-numbing monotony. By midday I had finally slugged back enough of the swill passing for coffee that I needed to relieve myself.

I strode down the hall to the lavatory, did what I needed to do, and was washing my hands when I glanced into the mirror above the sink. My eyes caught sight of something on the backside of my left shoulder, which had the color and consistency of oatmeal. Leaning into my reflection for a better look, I was aghast to realize that I'd spent the better part of the day walking around with a dried mound of cat vomit less than a foot from my face.

Had this gone unnoticed by my coworkers?

Their terminally torpid state made it believable enough they might have missed seeing my affliction. Or, perhaps they noticed the puke and were just apathetic about pointing out the upchucked accoutrement to my wardrobe, figuring if I didn't care about it, why should they? I began replaying every conversation I had that morning, trying to remember who had stood where while talking to me. Then I remembered I had driven in with Cole. How had she missed it? After cleaning myself up, I stormed from the bathroom, fuming, and called her to demand an answer.

"Your left shoulder, you say?" she asked. "That was on the far side from where I was sitting. You can't expect me to catch everything."

"I don't expect you to catch *everything*," I countered. "But I do expect you to notice if I'm walking around with vomit on my shoulder."

"*You* didn't catch it."

She had me there. It only made me madder, but it wasn't her fault. I hung up and came to the brooding realization that if you live without a mirror you've got to expect from time to time to not just end up with egg on your face, but puke on your apparel.

A mirror went up in our cabin that weekend.

GROSS GARMENTS ARE ONE THING, BUT THERE WERE OTHER OCCASIONS when I had to report for duty with a disfigurement to my actual person: one to the foot, the other to the face, both equally impossible for my coworkers to miss this time.

One of the injuries came after a battle with my mortal enemy: automotive mechanics. I valiantly try to keep all our vehicles—from four-wheelers, to our commuting car, to our dog truck—running. Unfortunately, this effort doesn't come naturally to me, nor do I find the task of spending hours hunched under a hood to be a labor of love.

The dog truck—a '99 Ford, diesel engine, maroon in color and "lightly used" as they say in advertisement parlance—particularly plagued and challenged me. On top of the impressive sum already on the odometer when we got the vehicle, we logged a lot of miles in it, and they weren't easy miles. When loaded with us, the dogs, sleds, and gear, we were hauling—on average—around 2,000 pounds, and we lugged that weight all around the state, multiple times, and even to Canada and back when Cole and the dogs ran the Yukon Quest.

All these miles meant a lot of maintenance and over the years I had replaced almost every major mechanical component on the dog truck, but my injury was specifically related to when I endeavored to swap out a dead battery for a new one. Normally this change-out is one of the easier tasks, since it requires little more skill than a few turns of the wrench on bolts holding the mounting bracket down, then taking off the terminals attached to the battery itself.

However, for those who've never replaced a battery, seemingly all of them are solid with lead and as heavy, dense, and easy to cart around as a cannonball. The battery for the dog truck was a real badass though, a fifty-pound whopper, which was a hefty amount when lifted out of the engine compartment, but downright colossal when it nearly cleaved off my big toe.

The mishap happened as soon as I returned home from the auto-parts store. I had the new battery in the extended-cab portion of my other pickup truck, but as usual had a handful of canine copilots with me. Apparently, on the long drive home from town, the dogs wrestling and jumping around the interior must have shifted the battery's position, tipping it against the door. The nanosecond I opened the cab, the battery hit my foot. No time to react. No time to process the event as it unfolded. I didn't even register it falling. I just felt immediate and excruciating pain.

The weighty automotive component landed such that one of the sharp edges along the side of the battery made contact first. My toe sustained substantial damage, even through a work boot. The nail sheared off, and what remained looked like raw hamburger. Within minutes the whole thing also swelled to twice the digit's normal size and turned a dark plum color. The dogs riding with me had bound out of the truck, and several others free-ranging in the front yard upon my arrival home all darted over at the obvious signs of distress, but not even the concerned licks to the face they generously doled out were enough to take my mind off my mangled phalange.

The wound bled incessantly and any attempt to slide my foot into a shoe failed and left me in racking pain. The next morning was agony to just cover it with a tube sock, which is precisely the burden I had to bare to limp my way into the office.

No one seemed to comprehend the monumental effort I made to show up at all when a lesser man might have called in sick (although to be fair, I think most of my coworkers had made the correlation of my shore leave being taken simultaneous to fresh snowfall occurrences, but that was neither here nor there on this morning). Rather than praising my herculean endeavor to avoid missing my shift, everyone focused on the foot itself, monitoring me discreetly from the corners of their eyes as I hobbled around the office on my heel and other good foot. I eventually made my way to my desk, wincing in pain with every step, and only having to explain what had transpired a handful of times while en route to my workspace. But, as anyone who has worked in an office knows, gossip moves at the speed of light.

Within a few hours our publisher and head honcho came around. A candidate for the Bad Boss Hall of Fame, I often compared him to sperm because most days there was only a one-in-a-million chance of him becoming human.

We were only graced with his presence in the newsroom on rare occasions, typically when he would come in to discuss a particularly controversial decision from a football game with one of the sports writers. Otherwise, like all reptiles, I assume he spent most of his time under a rock somewhere.

"Robert," he often got my name wrong, but in a Freudian way managed to recall part of my last name, "what's this I hear about you only wearing one shoe to work?"

"Yeah, sorry about that, had an accident over the weekend," I said.

"Well, we can't have you roaming the halls with one shoe, not professional. You know how it is," he tut-tutted.

"Sure, sure, I understand completely," I groveled insincerely, while absently stirring a cup of swill.

"How bad is the thing anyway?"

Until that point I had been craning my head to the side to talk with him, but since he asked, I wheeled my chair back and swung my foot around giving him a good look at the sopping, crimson-soaked sock covering the end of it. I had felt it bleeding slowly for hours while I slaved away at my desk. At the sight of it, his face blanched to as white as my tube sock had been when I left the house that morning.

"That," he swallowed audibly, seemingly choking back a dry heave, "looks pretty bad."

"Nah, I'm sure it'll wash right out," I said sardonically, and that ended all conversation, related to my foot or otherwise. With a slanted smile, I swiveled my chair back and resumed looking busy.

THAT SMASHED TOE, HOWEVER, WAS NOT THE WORST OF MY MUSHING related maladies. During a savage storm when bone-chilling temperatures combined with punishing gusts created a windchill of minus eighty-five degrees, I incurred a disfigurement that was even more challenging to conceal.

Cole and I had trucked north for the Gin Gin 200 in Paxson, Alaska, a place that would have to acquire a horse to even make the step up to being called a one-horse town. The weather made for a particularly brutal event that year. Several teams, ill-prepared for the severity of the Siberian-borne cold and stabbing winds, scratched from the race. Several others struggled to finish, but not unscathed; many mushers and dogs alike sustained frostbite.

We planned on being gone about a week—between travel time to and from, as well as the two days it would take Cole to race—so we decided to bring all our dogs, and I would put in a few training runs with the huskies that weren't slated to compete that weekend.

After the racers departed on the first day, I swaddled myself in my insulated snowsuit and goose down parka, and then ran the team about twenty-five miles out, where I found myself in the maw of a ground blizzard. The driving wind whirled snow past my face in white stripes moving so fast, it created a dizzying effect, like sticking your head out the window of a speeding car and looking straight down at the asphalt. The elements devoured me, although in that moment it felt more like they were smothering me. All my senses were snuffed out. There was no detail, no way to focus, and unlike the pleasant hum of rushing wind generated by a moving vehicle, the storm overpowered all sound with a deafening roar. The danger of these conditions, combined with the isolation of the situation, can—and did—create a sense of panic, similar in scale to being locked in a freezer.

The dogs marched forward while simultaneously leaning sideways to angle their bodies forty-five degrees to contend with the barrage of unceasing oblique wind. Thankfully, they had on their wind-cheating coats and other protective gear, but I worried: *Was it enough?* After all, I could feel powerful gusts cut like a razor blade through the seams of my many layers of clothing, stinging the skin underneath.

My niggling mind could ruin anything if given time to think about it long enough, but the risks of mushing farther into such inhospitable elements far outweighed any training rewards to be gained. I made the decision to turn the team around and began to mush back to the dog truck. Despite having my hooded ruff up, its face-hole cinched tight, and under it a fleece neck gaiter pulled up to just below my eyes, I felt my nose get painfully cold on the return trip, but it eventually numbed and stopped hurting. I considered the loss of feeling a good thing until I put the dogs away and went inside to warm up.

"What's wrong with your nose!" shouted a tactless woman at the bar upon seeing my face.

"I don't know, what?" I asked, sincerely.

"It's all white. Looks frostbit," she said.

I darted to the bathroom and worse than the odor of stale urine, my estranged friend, the mirror, revealed the impolite hag was correct. My nose remained intact, albeit absent of all natural color. Instead, it glowed ghostly white and bore a waxy appearance. I knew this wasn't good, and splashed warm water over my wind-burned beak, but there wasn't much else I could do except wait to see how bad it became.

As it turned out, I got pretty lucky. When the color returned, my nose turned an angry shade of red, swelled a bit, and felt sore to the slightest touch, but that appeared to be the worst of my ailments. No blackness, nothing necrotic. My personal diagnosis: I sustained more of a frostnip than an actual bite.

The real damage occurred a few days later when we got home. I hooked up the dogs for another training run and ran fifty miles in more moderate minus-thirty-degree weather. Balmy by comparison to the cold in Paxson, but I hadn't accounted for my burned tissue— exponentially more susceptible to freezing temperatures than normal, healthy skin.

Again, I had a neck gaiter over my face, and it protected the lower portion of my nose, but the bridge area right between my eyes did not fare as well. Halfway through the run I could feel it, itching at first, but by the end it seared like a hot match being stubbed out between my eyes. This time I was not so fortunate and within a day or two the severity of the burn manifested itself. My skin sloughed off like wet tissue and the meaty, granular texture beneath swelled and bled in a near constant trickle.

Since I'd used most of my vacation days for the year at the race, I once more soldiered into work. There was no concealing this wound, but I did my best to downgrade its appearance with a little bit of clever camouflage. I smeared burn cream all over my nose, which made me look more like a lifeguard than a reporter, but the greasy white balm reduced the gruesomeness of the open sore.

The publisher was by chance standing in the lobby when I arrived. After getting one glance at me, he exhaled a deep sigh, then with an annoyed look on his sagging face he asked, "What this time?"

I gave him the abbreviated version, since I knew—like all his workplace dialogue—he asked the question insincerely. Despite the brevity of my tale, it wasn't brief enough, and halfway through my spiel I felt a rivulet run down my cheek—a sure sign of my nose oozing liquid again.

"You, ah, you got something leaking there, Robert," he said, his upper lip curled in revulsion.

"Oops, sorry about that," I said, while dabbing a tissue to the source.

We then proceeded to stand in a silence more awkward for him than me for more than a minute, just blinking at each other—him utterly aghast and, I think, trying to comprehend what inside me was broken, and I just to indulge in his discomfort with the situation. Perhaps sensing my complete lack of willingness to say anything further, he eventually took his leave from our exchange without bidding me *adieu*.

It wasn't my proudest moment, and now, years later, my nose is still more sensitive to the cold than any other part of my body, but it's nothing compared to how tender the memories are from back when I used to humiliate myself, and gross out coworkers and bosses, during my days punching a time clock.

I'd be lying if I said I missed toiling away my days in an office environment. On the contrary, I'm elated to have broken the shackles of boardroom banality. No more uncomfortable exchanges with other employees, no more embarrassing clothing malfunctions, and best of all no more making sorry excuses to the hoofed demons who reign under the guise of "middle management," but make it blatantly obvious they actually worship Satan himself.

I am a disheveled dog owner, and I've accepted who and what I am. I'm OK with it because it has afforded me the freedom to spend all day around the dogs, which not only allowed for more lucrative training that paid dividends when Cole raced, but more importantly it enabled me to be here for our brood during critical moments. When a dog broke a collar, or other hardware that contains them to the yard failed, I was right there to run outside and catch them before they could quarrel with another dog, or, run miles away where they could be hit by a car or shot by a neighbor unfriendly to strays. When dogs were sick, I was available to administer necessary medications and apply ointments and salves, exactly when scheduled. When dogs grew elderly and some became feeble to the point of being frail, I was present to attend to their geriatric needs—carrying them outside to relive themselves, bringing the water bowl to them, and cooking and tearing into tiny pieces chicken and other dishes more digestible to old and sour stomachs. And most importantly, I was there when they finally succumbed to the great unknown. I could kneel by their sides, caress and comfort them as much as possible in those last moments, and unabashedly whisper into their ears how much they meant and how much I would miss them. None had to die alone.

Being home gave them all an enriched, full life, and on their terms. They never had to wait at home, longing for my return, as so many doting dogs are forced to do while their owners are away for an eight-hour work-day. In essence, my constant presence allowed for me to be who they needed me to be, while also allowing me to be the dog owner I always wanted to be.

Beyond caring for the dogs, freelancing from the house also permit-ted me to be a stay-at-home dad, and I have delighted in the duty of raising my daughter and instilling in her all the energy, empathy, and insanity that comes with living with forty dogs. Not only is being the *paterfamilias* the most rewarding and supremely satisfying job I've ever held, but Lynx is the only boss I answer to, and she only judges me if I've somehow man-aged to track poo in the house. But, as someone who most days washes her hands by letting the dogs lick them clean, and even occasionally exhibits puke on her own clothes, hers is a critique I can live with.

A Mean, Mischief-Making Monster

L OOK AT IT, SHAGOO! JUST LOOK AT IT!" I ADMONISHED, POINTING
at the homemade dessert she nearly ruined before Cole or I had even
a bite.

The culprit couldn't have been more clear, since there were no other
animals in the house that would have systematically licked all the cream-
cheese icing off of a two-tiered carrot cake, but still our perpetual problem
child plead the fifth as if advised by legal counsel.

Like always, Shagoo—a husky with a coat as villainously black as
her soul—distanced herself from the crime by crouching on the far side of
the room, the farthest point from the confection. She also sported what
I'm sure in her mind was an expression of innocence, but like an offender
feeling the anguish of their guilt, her body language betrayed her. Her ice-
blue eyes were a little too wide open, she panted nervously, and her tail
fluttered ever so slightly from anxiety.

I recognized her pantomime, having given the same performance at
work just days earlier when my boss walked up behind me while near the
climax of a salacious story. His reaction could be summed up the same as
Cole's response to Shagoo.

"This is unbelievable, even for you," she said.

Cole had a point. We were fairly used to Shagoo's skullduggery. In

Shagoo weaving between ice blocks washed ashore during winter.
Despite her serene appearance, I'm fairly confident this demon-dog
conducted séances while we were at work.

all honesty, it wouldn't have surprised me to find out she channeled dead people when we were away from home. In fact, that discovery would make some of her mischievous exploits more explainable, including this most recent one. She had truly outdone herself.

In the interest of full disclosure, from the day we got Shagoo she had always been a little feral, coming from a musher rumored to have experimentally bred a wild wolf with some of his kennel dogs in order to capitalize on their natural proclivity for covering hundreds of miles daily. Instead, he ended up with a ferocious litter, as inclined to bite someone trying to harness them as they were to run.

I never could get the musher to confirm if Shagoo was among his dogs with a recent infusion of wild genetics, but she sure acted the part. Her first night with us she bit our German shepherd, Tatika, a dog not only much larger and older than Shagoo, but also one with a kind and gentle soul that all our other dogs—particularly newcomers—seemed to immediately sense and take comfort in. Tatika had cautiously approached in an attempt to steal a cursory sniff of this stranger, and somehow this provoked Shagoo enough to lash out with a nip to Tatika's nose.

We scolded Shagoo immediately to let her know our home was not a domicile where domestic violence was tolerated, but the message seemed lost on her. To our dismay, over the next few weeks, months, and eventually years, Shagoo took a bite out of every dog we owned at least once. Dogs that were younger, older, smaller, larger, meaner, it didn't matter. The she-devil chomped on dogs that had threatened her, dogs that submitted to her, and dogs that didn't even know she was present until they felt her toothy fury.

Don't get me wrong, though, these weren't outright attacks. No, Shagoo never exhibited excessive savageness. She was more mean jerk than murderous psychopath, and the quick snaps she doled out appeared to be her attempting to exercise some perceived power, throwing her weight around so to speak, what little of it there was.

Shagoo's growth had been stunted, because like Coolwhip, she was a "wheezer," and suffered from the congenital condition of laryngeal paralysis. Shagoo could eat, but developed a wet, congested sound to her breathing afterward, an indication some food went down the wrong pipe. Also, walking her outside just a few yards to relive herself caused her to collapse, gasping for air, her tongue and gums turning purplish-blue.

Without surgery she wouldn't live long, but the musher who originally owned her admitted he didn't have the money to pay for the expensive procedure. A sad reality of the mushing world is that sometimes providing for the many outweighs providing for the one. The musher asked if I wanted her.

I discussed it with Cole and we slept on it overnight, but the next day Shagoo came home with us. After we got our initial glimpses of her personality, we named her Shagoo, after Mr. Magoo, a cantankerous cartoon character also short in stature. In retrospect, we probably should have gone with something more appropriate, like Tyson, Dahmer, or someone else notorious for nibbling on their own kind.

We splurged on surgery for Shagoo and afterward her breathing improved substantially, not enough to ever be a sled dog, but she could easily handle walks and short hikes. The procedure came with one complication, however. Over time—as the veterinarian predicted—scar tissue built up in Shagoo's throat, and her breathing became as audibly heavy as Darth Vader's. Even more off-putting, she developed a loud hack not unlike a patient with terminal emphysema. This resulted in her making the most unsettling noises several times an hour, and dozens of times over the course of a day. These disturbances sounded like the squeaking hinge of an old door being opened *very* slowly with a calamitous throat-clearing huff at the end, much like *eeeeeeeeeeeeeee-HUH!* Waking up to her haunting late-night wretches became a perpetual part of our existence, but one we begrudgingly learned to live with and occasionally sleep through.

Behaviorally, things also went from bad to worse after Shagoo's surgery, because with an almost fully open airway, she felt strong enough to menace at full strength. While small, she was spunky, and figured out early on that you don't have to be the toughest dog in the yard to rule, you just have to hold the visage of being the toughest, which she did. With each brief bout of bitchy aggression, she extended her authority, and quickly rose in power, becoming the Napoleon Bonaparte of our kennel. She even tried to extend her reign by threatening humans.

Shagoo didn't make this obvious like the typical dog advertising with aggressive overtures such as barking and lunging at unwelcome newcomers. Shagoo, as always, was a smooth criminal, often getting very close to guests, even attempting to rub against their legs and nuzzle them with her nose. But, if the person touched Shagoo back, she would immediately switch from Jekyll to Hyde and become very aloof and threatening to them. She particularly hated anyone violating the personal space around her head or face, and looking into her eyes, even briefly, sparked instantaneous rage.

Cole and I worked hard to keep this dark side of Shagoo's personality in check, and for the most part we were able to protect house guests with only a few lapses here and there, one of the most memorable coming after Cole completed her first Iditarod. We had invited a friend over who wanted to hear some tales from the trail, and she was someone quite fond of Shagoo. In previous brief visits, Shagoo had seduced this woman into believing the feeling was mutual.

By this time, we knew the tripwires that set Shagoo off, and did our best to dissuade anyone from detonating one of them. Our friend was lovingly stroking Shagoo's neck and back, and Shagoo acted innocently . . . oh so innocently. This duplicitous dog couldn't have pretended to be eating up the attention any more if she had a spoon.

We began drawing the line after Shagoo went beyond leaning in to receive more affection from our friend, and slowly began climbing up her lap to purportedly get more caressing.

"Don't encourage her too much," I warned. "I know how she seems, but trust me. You don't want to let that dog get too close to your face."

"Oh, it's OK," our friend said. "Shagoo and I are buddies. She just wants a few kisses."

At that, short of suffering scorching hemorrhoids, Cole and I couldn't have squirmed more uncomfortably in our seats, so *again*, I emphasized what a bad idea it would be to let Shagoo get too near to her jugular no matter how sugar sweet she portrayed herself.

"Really, its fine," our friend was starting to say, but Shagoo interrupted before she could finish her sentence. This dog, who just a split-second earlier had a puppylike innocence to her, now had a facial expression as savage as if suffering from full-blown rabies. Shagoo's ears were back tight against her head, her lips raised in a wrinkle of snout, her teeth clenched tightly and fully bared, and her whole body was quivering in a rage raw as red meat.

"What's wrong with her?" our friend asked through a gasp of terror, while slowly putting her hands up like she was being robbed at gunpoint.

"I warned you that she could be a little gauche with guests," I said, while Cole intervened more effectively.

"Shame! Get down from there," she scolded, and Shagoo immediately complied, slinking off to the other side of the room. There, from her dog bed, she gave one last defiant *eeeeeeeeeeeeeee-HUH* noise, and then resigned herself to glaring at us with a frustrated "you ruin all the fun" kind of look for the remainder of the evening.

As a pet parent, I've squandered far too many hours psychoanalyzing Shagoo's eccentricities. On the surface, her actions could be perceived as purposefully disruptive, attention-seeking behaviors, except that with incidents such as intimidating our friend, it always appeared Shagoo genuinely couldn't help herself. Little to nothing was done to provoke her aggression, per se, other than the attention she received was not on *her* terms.

This has led me to wonder if perhaps her mischievous manifestations weren't behavioral problems at all and instead were clinical symptoms of a true neuropsychological problem. The notion has been almost completely unexplored in pets, but I honestly believe that some dogs suffer from the same types of mental health disorders as humans, including possibly autism or schizophrenia. If so, then it is also fathomable that the same genetics that led to Shagoo's congenital breathing problem may have caused some form of undiagnosed mental health problem as well.

SHAGOO HAD MANY OTHER "ENDEARING" FACETS TO HER UNUSUAL personality other than just unprovoked hostility. She also channeled much of her obsessive-compulsive behavior into patrolling the borders of our property and bringing home the corpses of any interlopers found intruding on her turf. A mouser extraordinaire, I never minded seeing her trot home clenching in her jaws the dangling body of voles or other rodents she sniffed out before they stole from our winter cache of dog food, but it was a little more unsettling when she brought back larger quarry, such as grouse and snowshoe hare attempting to take refuge under the gnarled root balls of one of the wind-downed trees in our woodsy yard.

A few neighbors also raise and release game birds in the hope of having more species to hunt, despite the illegality of doing so. In spring, ring-necked pheasants show up sporting their gorgeous breeding plumage: cherry-red faces, iridescent green heads, and crisp white collars, as well as copper-and-gold breasts and body colors. Their rooster-like calls radiate from every corner of the yard, making it almost too easy for Shagoo to zero in on them.

Her most amazing kill, however, came after a knock-down, drag-out

Shagoo, exhausted from a tussle with one of the largest trespassers she ever took on—a feral turkey.

brawl with another species exotic to Alaska—released domestic turkeys, including some toms tipping the scales to twenty-five pounds, nearly as heavy as Shagoo.

Most of these birds stick close to the areas where they were released, since they continually get handouts from those who raised them, but one fall a male wandered a little too far off the reservation. We, Shagoo and I, were out splitting wood when between *ka-thunks* of my maul dropping on another dry piece of spruce, we heard a gobbler give a low, hoarse call from the forest at the front of our property.

Shagoo immediately went into high alert. She has sort of a beard-like mane that she can flare out when she's really excited, and it was flared to full extension. She stood still as a statue, staring in the direction of the sound, her ears the only things moving and tracking like two satellite dishes honing in on a signal. Moments later, the bird cried again and Shagoo dashed off, a black blur speeding toward the sound.

Seconds later I could hear the thrashing of brush, excited rasping from Shagoo, and clucks of alarm from the turkey. I hastened in the direction of the ruckus to ascertain who had the upper hand. The scene I found reminded me of a cartoon panel out of the Sunday funny pages: just a cloud of dust as the two rolled around on top of each other. Shagoo bit at the bird and attempted to hold it in her paws, while the tom chopped with its wings and kicked at Shagoo with the sharp, bony spurs on the back of its heels. They were locked in mortal combat.

I wanted to intervene, since it looked as though Shagoo may have literally bitten off more than she could chew this time, but before I made a move, the battle royale ended. Shagoo struck a death blow. Using her jaws, she snapped down on the turkey's fleshy, featherless neck and didn't let go until it stopped moving. Shagoo then dropped the dead bird and collapsed by her kill to catch her breath, her chest heaving in billows, and little tufts of her fur and the bird's loose feathers floating all around her. She looked totally spent, and almost, but not quite too tired to emit a triumphant *eeeeeeeeeeeeeeee-HUH.*

I wasn't sure what to do. I didn't necessarily think it appropriate to praise Shagoo for killing another creature, but at the same time I was happy she had taken down a bird that in all likelihood could and would outcompete our native grouse species. Instead, without saying a word, I picked up the plump-breasted tom and brought it in the house. There I cleaned and plucked the bird, and cooked it for dinner. Thanksgiving was still a few weeks away, but I've always hated waste, and the fat fowl made for a flavorful autumnal meal. I did feel a little guilty claiming Shagoo's catch, but she has since paid me back, many times over, by stealing meals from me through the years.

GETTING BACK TO THE GREAT CAKE CAPER, THE ZENITH OF SHAGOO'S food-snatching skills, we were well aware of how sly she could be when it came to swiping a meal we'd made for ourselves. I've seen mountain goats that were less nimble than Shagoo when it came to climbing on counters, and she was equally capable when it came to opening cupboards and getting into the garbage. Often after a dinner disappeared—say the last slice of pizza—Cole and I would only learn the true fate of our food after pointing fingers at each other.

"You didn't eat it?" I'd ask.

"No! Are you telling me you didn't either?" Cole would ask, and then we'd know.

"Shagoo," we'd say in unison.

She was incredibly calculating, but smart enough to know when to go off script, too, such as when Cole or I stepped out of the room, and she knew she had mere seconds to successfully swipe something. Once, after making a savory meal of moose steaks and baked potatoes, I stepped outside to pluck some fresh-grown chives from our herb patch. I couldn't have been gone longer than thirty seconds, but in that time Shagoo had not only snatched my steak down from the stove top, but in doing so had also pawed open the oven door and accidentally twisted on two of the surface burners to full bore (I presume while her paws fumbled over the dials as she committed grand theft dinner). Had I been gone more than a few seconds, it's entirely possible the roaring blue flames could have ignited any number of dishrags, paper towels, and other flammable items in the kitchen, and burned down our entire cabin.

Her getting to our from-scratch carrot cake was the pinnacle of all Shagoo's pilfering though. We had never attempted one before, instead using the garden-grown goodies as casserole ingredients, side dishes, or for nibbling between meals, but a perk of long summer days is an increase in natural sugars for crops like carrots, so we decided to commit an entire Saturday to creating the carrot-flavored confection.

We started in the morning, pulling up the slender orange veggies from the earthy beds, laboriously washing them, peeling them, shredding them by hand over the course of the day, and eventually baking them into two, thick, spongy rounds. For hours the heavenly aroma filled our cabin, building our anticipation. After they came out of the oven and cooled, Cole completed the mouthwatering masterpiece by smothering the two-tiered cake in gooey, homemade, cream-cheese frosting.

After finishing our dinner we were looking forward to having a slice of our *pièce de résistance* with childlike enthusiasm, but wanted to let our palates clear to truly appreciate what we had spent the day making, so we decided to tackle the evening dog chores first. Knowing Shagoo's knack for being naughty, we put the cake on top of the refrigerator—a height just inches below the ceiling—to be sure there was no chance our furred felon could ruin the sweet culmination of our meal.

Still, she found a way.

We were able to deduce her method from the trail of thrashed kitchen debris she knocked to the floor in her wake. In the twenty minutes, at most, that we were outside, Shagoo had leapt several feet, from the back of an easy chair, to land on a countertop. There she proceeded to walk across the stove, jump the sink, climb up a pantry shelf next to the fridge, and then must have carefully balanced on a coffeemaker while standing on her hind legs and tiptoes to get to the cake.

Here's the ridiculous part: she didn't eat the cake. She couldn't. Already stretching precariously just to reach it, she must not have been able to gain enough of an angle to take a bite out of the cake. Instead she settled for licking off all of the frosting as far as her tongue could reach.

When we returned to the cabin my eyes immediately went to the cake, and seeing orange color where white icing should have been, I knew we were screwed. Upon closer inspection, we found two-thirds of the cake was bare. She had even used her nose to nudge the top tier of the cake over a few inches after she had licked it clean, to tongue out as much of the middle layer of icing as she could reach.

While we were incensed about the cake, and had to make an outward showing of disapproval, I'd be lying if I said I didn't secretly applaud Shagoo's ingenuity and admire her tenacious spirit. She was brilliant in her duplicity, right down to the completion of her Oscar-worthy performance of acting as though she had nothing to do with any of the wrongdoing.

This act, much like Shagoo herself, wasn't just quirky; that was something I was used to. For years I worked with a guy who considered himself a karaoke connoisseur, and with the veins on the side of his head bulging and the corners of his mouth foaming, he would rant for hours about how drunk guys who sang Britney Spears songs to the amusement of their friends "didn't really get the craft." That's quirky, but Shagoo was far more than that.

She was eccentric, but not haphazardly crazy. She had wits, could be meticulous with her planning, and showed a single-mindedness that I couldn't help but find inspiring. She knew what she wanted, and she never let anything stand in her way, and I think because of this particular personality trait, I even envied Shagoo a little. We all have deeply held desires in our life—perhaps possessions we long to own, exotic places we hope to "one day" visit, or people we want to be honest or intimate with but lack the words.

We often settle for less for any number of reasons, not the least of which is lacking the courage to take a chance, but Shagoo was not bound by the self-consciousness that afflicts human egos. She lived life in the now, seized every day, was governed wholly by her id, and while much mischief resulted from her incontrovertibly unique personality, so did treasured memories. She may have technically been our dog, but her whole being screamed, "I'm still going to be me," and because of her untamable, true-to-herself ethos, she has forever earned a special place in my heart.

From Muskrats to Moose

A DARKNESS, LIKE BEING IN THE BOWELS OF A BEAR'S WINTER den, had settled on us several hours earlier. Even the stars seemed smothered that evening, and only the narrow beam of our headlamps broke the black of winter's night, which made the bloodcurdling shriek that came from the front of our team even more chilling than the thirty-below temperature.

"Can you see what happened?" Cole shouted.

"Not a thing," I said. "We gotta get up there."

I was riding in the sled bag while Cole drove the team, which came to a literal screeching halt. I blanched with thoughts of the numerous terrible scenarios that could have transpired. We were on a far-flung section of trail where the trunks of trees burned by an 80,000-acre wildfire in 1969 still stood blackened and forlorn. We rarely used this area due to the track being a favorite stomping ground of trappers, but the sweeping expanse enticed us by being one of the few locales with mushable trails in a winter with scant snowfall.

We couldn't immediately tell what occurred because in temperatures that cold, whenever the team stops, the heat from the dogs' warm bodies and panting breaths creates a visually impenetrable ice fog. All we could detect through the dense cloud of steam were the jerky movements of what seemed like dogs in distress near the front. The pack behind them looked back at us, their eyes reflecting our headlamp light in gleaming greens and reds, like old flash photography.

We feared the worst. A dog must have veered off the trail to dip a mouthful of snow and stepped into the deadly gear set either by a back-woodsman, one of a handful of folks still eking out their living from killing furbearing animals, or, more likely, hardware left lurking by a trapper-wannabe looking to emulate this bygone lifestyle.

This horror happens at least once a year to some unlucky pet around the state. In the worst-case scenario the dog's neck breaks instantly from the force of the trap's steel jaws slamming shut. In the best case, the trap may not immediately crush anything vital, and the dog's owner is granted a few seconds to free their beloved friend before the immense pressure on the pet's neck and windpipe cuts off the supply of oxygen and it suffocates.

Freeing a dog is tougher than it sounds. The traps have rigid springs that apply hundreds of pounds of pressure, so the jaws can't be pried open; rather the springs on the side must be compressed. The easiest way is to stand on the jaws while squeezing the springs, but with soft snow beneath the trap, and holding on with gloved or mittened hands, it can take minutes to open one with a writhing animal in it.

"Quick, quick, quick!" I yelled.

Cole set the snowhooks and we both sprinted to the front as fast as we could. We were horrified by the bloody spatters sullying the virgin snow and depicting the violent tragedy in vibrant detail. Mere seconds had passed since the team stopped, but by the time we got to the swing dogs, Butterscotch and Squirrel were locked in a tug of war over what was left of a snowshoe hare. One dog had the head in its mouth, complete with long ears clenched in its molars. The other female had a portion of fuzzy white hide and pink ribcage clamped in her jaws, and each was pulling and growling, attempting to get the remainder of the poor—and now lifeless—creature away from the other.

Phew was my first thought. *Gross* my immediate second.

Judging from some of the frozen red clumps of ice and blood around the mouths of the leaders, it looked like a few other dogs were also involved in the melee, but had gulped down the evidence in the brief time it took us to get to them. It was a shocking scene, but not entirely surprising. Sled dogs have all the prey-chasing instincts of any pack of wild canines, combined with a voracious appetite that is perpetually trying to meet the demands of their hyperactive metabolism.

Usually, one of the best parts about mushing, other than the time spent with the dogs themselves, is the uncountable number of hours we deliberately wander through wilderness. There, we have witnessed soul-moving spectacles of wildlife that otherwise would not have been encountered, but the hideous interaction presenting itself left me with mixed emotions. Sure, I felt blessed none of my dogs fell victim to metal jaws, but I bemoaned the life lost to their canine jaws. Nobody wants to see one of their best friends with a mouthful of bunny.

However, life with forty dogs has taught me on multiple occasions that nature is always playing for keeps. Life in Alaska is a harsh existence for all of us, but for animals especially it is a dog-eat-dog world (or in this case dog-eat-hare). I had to remind myself, my dogs' actions weren't done out of malevolence or maliciousness. The act was simply two animals driven by their primeval desires, and, as someone who's drawn to the outdoors myself—and the company of canines more than my own kind—I know how difficult that call of the wild is to resist.

THIS HARE WAS THE MOST GRUESOME EXAMPLE OF OUR DOGS CATCHING a hapless creature, but not the only one. While conditioning a team one particularly wet fall, when our normal four-wheeler training trails began to look like a series of Venetian canals more than dirt paths, and small animals suffered flooding from their usual abodes, I noticed something weird and dark dangling from the mouth of my swing dog.

Zoya, an all-white female with chocolate-brown eyes, had always been preoccupied. She had talent, to be sure. Zoya could lead when asked and her fitness was never in doubt, but she always seemed to be looking sideways down trail intersections and driveways, *every* one, and thinking about other things while running. She wasn't consumed by the rhythm of work like most other dogs. Zoya's air was the same as an office worker who really likes their vocation and knows their trade well, yet still spends much of the day slinking onto social media sites or sneaking personal calls. She just needed more entertainment than her job offered, and on this day she found it.

Unlike the hare, where numerous dogs involved themselves to the point of the team coming to a standstill, Zoya had stealthily nabbed her prize without the other dogs detecting anything. I too never saw her overtly lunge or even move furtively in any way. It was a complete mystery when and how she seized the small creature.

I stopped the team and sloshed up to her through the ankle-deep water curious as to what she had. Most of the dogs' wet-season catches had consisted of voles and field mice, and this was larger than both, but too plump to be a marten or any member of the weasel family.

As I reached Zoya, her tail swished with self-satisfaction and she made no attempts to hide her plaything, or gulp it down as is more common. Instead she held her head high, while still breathing hard from the exercise, her nostrils flaring twice as hard as usual to compensate for her teeth clenched tight on the lifeless, brown lump of fur.

"Give it here, Zoya," I said, and, surprisingly, without a fight she relinquished.

My leather-gloved hand received a muskrat—an oily rodent with a round, ratlike tail, rather than a flat, leathery one like its bucktoothed relative the beaver.

"Sorry, little guy," I said, before walking it off the trail a few yards and placing it at the base of a tree. It seemed like an appropriate, albeit impromptu, final resting spot. As with the rabbit, I wasn't proud my dogs had killed a wild creature attempting to survive in the already harsh natural world, but I was thankful for two things: its death had been swift and it hadn't harmed any of my canine companions when it left this world.

SAFETY IS ALWAYS A CONCERN FOR DOG OWNERS, AND SOMETIMES IT'S the dogs that stand to lose more from a beastly encounter, as I learned during one particularly close call while on an early morning run before work. In fall, when at the height of our competitive goals, we used to get up around 5:00 a.m., before sunrise and when the temperature was still cool. In the darkness and falling drizzle, we'd attempt to get in a few miles before work. We had a loop about five miles long we ran with two twelve-dog teams pulling our four-wheelers, and this day we were only about half a mile into the circuit when we found ourselves in a prickly situation.

The path took a long descent down a steep hill, then turned ninety degrees in a hard-right onto the shore of a black sand beach bordering the east side of Cook Inlet. As is common with these types of turns, the leaders and front few dogs behind them go out of view until we round the corner a few seconds later.

However, when we rounded the bend, we could just see a mass of about six dogs all heaped together like a NASCAR crash. All that was missing was an official waving a yellow caution flag. We dismounted our respective wheelers, and ran to the front of the forward-most team. We expected the jumble to have resulted from one of the leaders stopping to poop, and then the swing and other following dogs tangling the lines as they inadvertently ran past them. A semi-common occurrence, simple to sort out.

Simplicity did not grace us with its presence.

As we got to the front end, Seeker, a floppy-eared gray-and-tan female who was in swing, had a porcupine the size of a suitcase pinned to the ground. Despite the thick beard of quills she already had sticking out of her face, she continued to bite the animal in a state of jaw-snapping hysteria.

Seeker had always been the exact opposite of delicate or dainty. She was a strong and sinewy dog that did everything to the tenth power. The tougher trail conditions got, the better she seemed to like them. This tenacious spirit made her a great racer, but in that early morning moment her manic excitement also made a bad situation much worse.

With leather gloves on, I was able to wrestle the spiky beast away from her, and sent it waddling on its way, minus its major defense system, but otherwise no worse for the wear. Then, under the dimness of our two tiny headlamps, Cole and I assessed the damage to our dogs. The front five all had taken quills. Goliath and Pong, who were in lead, only had a few in their wet black noses and leathery front paws. They must have pounced on the porcupine, but then, feeling the sting of its defenses, yielded before taking a bite. The predicament appeared the same for Screamer and Penny, two females who were right behind the swing position. They had only been impaled by a few quills each.

Seeker was a total mess though. She had hundreds of black-and-beige-colored quills in her nose and muzzle, in her gumline, and so many in the roof of her mouth and tongue that she couldn't close her jaws. Dozens more lined her forelegs and front paws, top and bottom. Still heavily panting from running and the thrill of the carnage she helped create, we worried she might have inhaled a few down her throat.

This was a dangerous situation on many fronts. The quills themselves cause immediate pain and damage, but also the same barbed shape that makes them stick in can also make them migrate farther and farther into the body within hours. On other occasions, we've seen dogs that have gotten them in their paws—either undetected, or quills already too deep to pull out—move all the way through, painfully popping out the top of the foot after several days. We've known other mushers who had dogs die when the tiny quills in the neck and chest migrated deep into the body and punctured vital organs or caused massive internal infections.

"There's no running her home like this," I said to Cole. "These quills have to be pulled out of her, right here, right now."

Having had other dogs get stuck with the needlelike spines before, we knew a difficult task lay ahead. In the past the procedure had usually taken the better part of an hour to get them all out, while working in the comfort and bright lights of our living room, with an assortment of plucking tools at our disposal, and never facing as many quills as Seeker suffered.

Not only were we in the rain and darkness, with the soft wet sand of the beach coating us as we wrestled with the dogs, but we initially feared the knives we carried on our waist belts were the only instrument we had to pull quills. Astonishingly though, after frantically rifling through the tool kit that came with the four-wheeler, we found a pair of puny pliers to work with.

Adding to the calamity, we had two entirely fresh and enthusiastic twelve-dog teams, one of them still parked precariously on a treacherous downhill slant. The dogs were all going berserk, their barking not only drowning out the sounds of ocean waves crashing just feet away from us, but their cacophony also making verbal communication between Cole and me nearly impossible despite standing practically face to face.

Some of the racketeers also began chewing neck lines out of the frustration of being stopped, and we wondered how long until one started in on the main gangline. Severing this umbilical cord between wheeler and team, we knew, would set the whole frenzied bunch running down the beach without either of us.

Without speaking, we commenced working as quickly as we could. I restrained Seeker by the neck and back of the head as Cole plucked the quills out of the dog's mouth as quickly as she could, trying to fling them far enough away from the team that when we got going again, no one else would be harmed. There were so many barbs in such dense clusters, she was able to yank four or five out at a time. Efficient, but painful to our pin-cushioned patient.

The only thing that we had going for us was, whether out of being in a state of shock or coming down from the adrenaline high she had just been on, Seeker seemed to understand we were trying to help. Her wide eyes with dilated pupils watched Cole's every move, but otherwise she remained mostly still. We had probably three-quarters of the quills—hundreds of them—out of her before she finally started getting squirmy, at which point I wrestled into a position basically sitting on top of Seeker to immobilize her for the few minutes more Cole needed to get the rest out.

We then moved on to the other lesser casualties, the entire ordeal taking close to an hour, but feeling much more like several days. We plucked the final few quills just as the first light of day was breaking on the horizon.

"What now?" I asked, dripping with sweat. The question rhetorical. Due to the setback, I knew we were on the verge of being late for work. Still, Cole somberly stated the obvious, "There's nothing we can do. We've got to turn the teams around and head for home."

This is exactly what we did, an astounding feat in itself since all the dogs were still full of adrenaline and mad out of their minds to run more. Cole and I on the other hand were completely on empty, drained of not just energy but also the normal flesh color of our faces. Back at the kennel we mustered the strength to put all the dogs away, feed them, and then head in for an eight-hour day. Feeling more dead than alive, I confess it was not my most productive day at the office.

SEEKER'S RUN-IN WITH THE PORCUPINE WAS DANGEROUS, BUT NOT OUR closest brush with dog death due to an unexpected encounter with wildlife. For this infamous title, the largest member of the deer family still reigns supreme. Moose, weighing more than 1,000 pounds and with long legs capable of stomping and kicking with the force of a sledgehammer, are by far the species we least want to see while on the trail.

Most mushers can tell tale of at least one close call with moose, but a few unfortunate souls have known worse, as happened to a neighbor of ours while mushing on a trail just a few miles behind our kennel. It was February, a time when the snow depth feels bottomless, and the giant ungulates are at their hungriest from winter's sparse offerings. Rather than wading through the deep powder, it takes fewer calories to walk on the trails the dogs and sleds have packed down hard for months, so the moose are on them in droves and don't want to yield when they see an oncoming dog team.

As relayed to me by this musher, his team came upon a crotchety female moose and while he halted his pack, the cow was not appeased and began stomping dogs. The brown behemoth made pass after pass through the team, each time sending shrieks of pain resonating into the air, and another downed dog left in its wake. Armed with nothing more than a cell phone and a snowhook, the musher gathered up the dogs at his feet as best he could, called his wife to come with a gun, and stood defensively swinging his snowhook in lasso fashion until she arrived. In the end, his lead dog lost its life and several others were nearly crippled.

Cole and I have been much more fortunate. Out of the scores of run-ins we've had with moose, we've only had two occasions where they went through the team intending to cause bodily harm to one or more dogs. One incident was on the same trail where our neighbors' team was attacked, but a few years later. We weren't far from the kennel, only about

*Over the years, we've encountered a lot of wildlife while running the dogs,
but sometimes the animals came to us. Moose visit the kennel so frequently
that most of the dogs barely take notice of them, as Oaky illustrates by
ignoring this large cow grazing just feet from her.*

a mile or two as the raven flies. The moose must have been browsing just
off the packed path and become startled by the sudden and silently moving team that appeared next to it.

I heard the crash of a branch breaking as the moose ran out from
the trees and cut through the team behind the swing dogs. The moose's
head was down, its ears back, and it had the exaggeratedly high step of an
animal deliberately trying to stomp. Amazingly it missed everyone, but
had we been moving just a hair faster or slower, the story might have been
entirely different.

On the other occasion we bumped into a moose it was an even closer call. We had just pulled the hook to leave the yard. Our exit trail runs about 200 yards through thick spruce and cottonwood trees before taking a soft ninety-degree turn onto a common-use mushing trail. When we first start out, even with our feet on the sled brakes, we're still speeding at close to twenty miles per hour, and as with the porcupine incident, there isn't much seeing around the corners with a seventy-foot-long string of dogs.

Once again, I was in the bag and Cole was driving and we were in the process of rounding the corner when a large cow moose trotted through the middle of the team. Instinctively, Cole stomped the brake bar, driving its spiked teeth deep into the snow, bringing us to a halt. As we came to a stop we saw the cow crane her muscular neck around to get a better look. Her huge body followed seconds later. It was clear from the look in her wide eyes that she intended to make another pass through our team.

Cole and I both began yelling "NO . . .NO . . . NO!" Without thinking I came out of the sled like a tightly coiled spring. I began running up the team waving my arms. My reaction so fast, I forgot to grab my only defensive weapon—the ax we always carried to clear downed deadfall from the trail—and left it back in the sled.

I darted up the line of dogs, quickly closing the amount of real estate between the cow and myself when out of the corner of my eye I detected movement to my left on the other side of the team. It was the cow's calf, standing nearly as tall as I was, but not moving toward or away from the team.

Mama moose and I both knew nothing was going to dissuade her from getting back to that baby.

"Easy, big girl," I said, but still she bolted back through the team, stomping with purpose. I saw the head of an orange-and-white dog jerk toward the ground, then its whole body go flying. It was Hildy, a sweet-heart of a dog we had raised from birth, and I was sure she had been kicked. I ran to her, still yelling at the top of my lungs and gesticulating like a madman, but not taking my eyes off the moose, which once reunited with its calf seemed as eager to get away from us as we were to see them go.

Cole had the snowhooks set and was also up to Hildy at this time.

"How bad is it?" she asked.

I ran my hands over her whole body, manually turning her head and bending her joints. To my utter amazement, she hadn't been kicked and was no worse for the wear.

"She's all right. I think we're all right," I said to calm myself as much as Cole.

Apparently as the moose went through, it had only stomped on Hildy's neck line. When it did, the force was great enough to pop the brass snap at the end of it into two pieces, freeing Hildy enough to allow her to dive out as far as her much longer tug line would allow and not be clobbered by the kicky moose.

With frayed lines, and even more frayed nerves, we turned the team around and put everyone away. After the adrenaline high faded we instead opted to take out the chain saws and thin out enough trees and brush on the corner to increase visibility, and make rounding it a little safer for everyone involved.

I'VE LEARNED THROUGH EXPERIENCE THE BEST WAY TO SOLVE PROBLEMS and cohabitate with moose is to learn to understand the animals' behavior and recognize what their motivation is. What is it that they need or want that is causing the dilemma in the first place?

Moose on the trail are one thing, we know what they want—the right of way. With no alternative paths to take, we're forced to take the risks of sharing space, but mitigate those risks by relinquishing a trail when possible. Back in the dog yard, where moose still pass through or come in search of whatever sparse fodder they can find, I've learned an equally gentle approach is the best way to solve problems.

This lesson was nearly learned at the expense of a dog. When we first set up our kennel, we took the advice of other mushers, all of whom had a zero-tolerance policy for moose anywhere near their dog yards.

"I keep a snapper raffle right by the door and you should too," one brazen old-timer told me (although I'm not sure a rusted Winchester counts as a sniper rifle).

I've never been keen on killing animals merely for trying to find food in the only environment they had ever known. In my opinion, the moose were here first, and it's not their fault I put up a cabin in the middle of their dining area. Still, I knew I had to protect my dogs, so I settled on ordering some rubber slugs for my twelve-gauge shotgun for any moose that got a little too close for comfort.

I discovered that while bouncing a rubber projectile off a moose's rear end stung enough to get them to temporarily leave, before long they would return and continue to do so daily for weeks, because they *needed* the food that was in my yard to survive. They couldn't and wouldn't be dissuaded.

However, after the hazing, the moose were always on edge. They acted more irritable and had a much shorter fuse when receiving even the slightest harassment from the dogs. One cow came back so ornery, as soon as the closest dog to her came out of his box to bark, the moose immediately went into a rage. The dog, a bold-spirited male named Bully, realized the danger of the situation and dove into his house to avoid being kicked, and even then the cow reared up and stomped a hole in the roof of Bully's box.

After that we stopped hazing and began simply monitoring the moose. I still carried a shotgun for the dogs, and my own, protection, but I never fired it again. To my surprise, the moose became much less dangerous.

They would come into the yard, even get right up to the edge of the dogs' living areas, but they peacefully ate what they needed—the willow that thrives on the periphery—which subsequently removed that resource from the area and their interest in pursuing it. They would then push on, rather than lingering about for weeks.

Furthermore, the dogs, possibly upon seeing our more relaxed stance with the moose, or perhaps reading the ungulates own more-relaxed body language, also ceased harassing the moose. On one occasion I even witnessed a moose mosey in with such gangly grace, and the kennel react with such nonchalance, that as the large cow passed one dog, she casually paused and the two briefly touched snouts, each taking in great curious nosefuls of the other's scent. The scene stirred in me the same emotions as the first time I laid eyes on God and man touching fingers in Michelangelo's *The Creation of Adam*. I couldn't help but be filled with serenity, and I savored every second of that rare, fleeting, and one could even argue divine moment between two species that are more typically antagonistic to one another.

And so it went for years. Other than the initial "intruder" bark to announce when a moose first came into view, the dogs quickly lost interest, quieted down, and got in their houses and went to sleep, leaving the moose to munch willow in peace. And peace is a good thing, from muskrats to moose to mushers, and all creatures between.

A Broken Limb but Never a Broken Spirit

THE PROGNOSIS LINGERED, AND WAS ABOUT AS WELCOME, AS POO tracked in on a shoe. With intense yet careful physical therapy, Wolf would gain full mobility again, but his days as a sled dog were believed to be over. The veterinarian's exact words were "he would never run again."

Here's the thing about sled dogs, though—they have a way of pulling off mind-blowingly impossible feats, at least when given the opportunity. Taking in huskies from other mushers and the pound, we've seen a lot of dogs that were given up on—or never given a chance at all—go on to become athletes of the highest caliber. But no dog came as far or demonstrated the truly indelible spirit of the sled dog like Wolf.

We liked Wolf long before he ever merged into our amalgamation of mutts. Living in Kasilof, Alaska—an area with half a dozen other mushers and roughly 300 dogs within a few square miles of our home—we got to know some of the dogs from other kennels. Sometimes it resulted from recognizing the same faces running in front of other mushers' teams when having head-on passes on the trail, or from word of mouth about which dogs in their kennel these folks think are showing signs of becoming their next rising star. In Wolf's case, tragedy brought him to our attention one late fall evening.

We had just gotten home from one of our own training runs when the phone rang. On the other end of the line, a friend relayed to us that a few miles down the road, a speeding car had slammed into a fellow musher's team.

"It's bad, really bad," said the friend who came upon the scene on her way home from work. "Several dogs are dead, some are severely injured and being rushed to the emergency clinic, and the ones that weren't hit need to be taken home."

I said we'd come immediately, then hung up and stared without expression at Cole.

"What? What is it?" she asked, reading my face.

Minutes passed before I could speak. My heart ached thinking of this musher and his dogs. A deep, spine-tingling fear pulsed through my body. I had always operated under the notion that all the dogs starting a run with me would come home alive, an idea as natural to me as accepting air into my lungs. Now I choked on my naivety.

No greater fear lurks in the minds of mushers than having a dog team run over by a motor vehicle. Yet, each year, even in Alaska, the areas we live become increasingly more urban, which makes crossing roads and driveways an unavoidable part of all mushers' attempts to perpetually eke out enough training miles to stay competitive.

It's a numbers game, really, and we do our best to increase the odds for our teams' safety. Many mushers, ourselves included, wear reflective clothing, splice in reflective material to the gangline, and add reflective patches to the dogs' harnesses for better visibility at night. Most mushers also avoid running at peak traffic times when motorists are commuting to or from work, or on Friday nights when people may be heading home after having a few drinks with dinner or at the bar.

Despite taking these precautions, several other factors combined to create the catastrophe that befell Wolf and his teammates. The musher had returned, that same day, from a weeklong vacation and despite being weary from the long flight, he felt the calling to pursue his passion. The dogs, having not run in far too long, were equally amped to go.

Without snow blanketing the trails, dog teams were still pulling four-wheelers for training. In the fading pink light of the day, the musher had hooked up two twelve-dog teams, driving the lead team himself while his handler's team eagerly chased. They decided on a loop only a few miles long, just enough to satiate everyone's desires, but their return path involved a highway crossing at the bottom of a steep, quarter-mile hill.

The musher crossed, but then eyeballed the oncoming headlights of a vehicle cresting the top. Not wanting to take chances in case the motorist was speeding, as people in this area often do, the musher signaled to his handler to hold up on the other side of the road.

However, the second team could not be dissuaded from their pursuit.

It's always difficult to contain the fervor of a sled-dog team and bring them to a stop, and the only thing dogs like more than running is chasing, which the huskies in that second team were doing.

The handler, who later recounted to me the situation from his perspective, said he did his best to set the front and back brakes, but the power and enthusiasm of this team—in their prime and having sat idle for seven days—could not be restrained. They went wild from the sight of their kennelmates pulling ahead and became deliriously committed to crossing the twenty-foot-wide asphalt divide.

Hurling themselves forward, they began to build momentum, and with each synchronized thrust they moved a few yards farther into the road. Within seconds, more than half the string of dogs spread across the paved surface, their bred-in desire about to become their downfall.

The driver admitted in testimony later that at the time his focus had momentarily shifted to fumbling with the radio. He never even slowed down. He bombed into the front half of the team, violently launching dogs through the air. Six dogs were struck. Two died at the scene. Two others were rushed to a veterinarian (but died the next day as a result of their extensive injuries). Amazingly, one dog, thrown just right, had no physical injuries. And one dog was struck and thrust so forcefully that his connecting tug line snapped. Free from the main gangline and scared out of his wits from the trauma he had endured, this dog, Wolf, ran away into the darkness of night.

Two years old at the time, Wolf had never been much of a people person, even before this accident. A very traditional-looking husky, Wolf's raven-black coat contrasted sharply with his white eyebrows, muzzle, chest, and socks. His glacier-blue eyes equally stood out from his ebony mask, making it obvious—and a bit disconcerting to newcomers—how watchful and wary he is around people he doesn't know.

Like many mushers who live away from the hustle and bustle of city life, Wolf's original owners lived off the grid, rarely having more than a handful of close friends stopping by, so Wolf and his littermates developed some antisocial tendencies. Not gregarious, as sled dogs go, his demeanor further complicated his situation after being struck by the speeding car.

As Wolf fearfully fled the chaos of the scene, in the dim light of his owner's headlamp beam, it appeared clear one of his hind legs sustained severe damage and in all likelihood was broken. The musher did his best to call Wolf back, but, far too frightened, he refused to return anywhere close to the site of the accident. With so many other dogs needing immediate care, the musher knew he would have to come back for Wolf, or, perhaps more appropriately, he hoped Wolf would come back to him.

By the time we arrived, the uninjured dogs had already been transported back to their kennel. The musher had scrambled to care for his still-living companions, but now came the sobering reality of dealing with the dogs that died doing what they loved. As I stepped from my truck, in the sparse light of my headlamp the first thing I noticed were my friend's eyes. They were bleary from wiping away tears.

Through sheer will he endured, but hollower, like a shell of the musher I knew. Having your heart pierced will do that, I supposed. I hugged him in a brother's embrace and whispered, "I'm sorry." The words were barely audible over the gently blowing wind, but not because I meant them to be. My voice, like my psyche, had retreated far inward as the fear that this could have been my team continued to churn in my mind.

After doing my best to briefly comfort him, we turned to the excruciating task at hand. The dead dogs lay still as stones. I stood silently and watched steam from the musher's breath billow into the night air as he mustered the strength to lift the first one into the bed of my truck.

"Do you want me to do this?" I asked.

"No," he said curtly, and I took no offense.

"I can do it," he declared, and he did.

THE NEXT DAY, WITH THE OTHER DOGS DEAD OR STABILIZED, THE musher resumed his search efforts for Wolf, but didn't have to go far. Despite only being able to use three legs, Wolf had traveled several miles to return home. His owner found him curled up on some spare flakes of straw left outdoors, not far from a previously full bucket of dog food he had tipped over. While good news that Wolf came back and clearly had an appetite, the damage to his lower leg looked worse than initially feared. The musher judged it completely smashed. Below the thick muscles of the upper thigh, the dog's leg had the appearance of an empty sock, the skin stretched loose and hollow, while below, closer to the paw, Wolf's ankle looked like there was a large bent spring stuffed inside.

His owner rushed him to the veterinarian and X-rays confirmed the severity of the break. Wolf required transport to an orthopedic specialist in Anchorage, a few hours north, and there his ankle was reconstructed. Numerous metal plates and screws had to be utilized to hold everything in place.

While the vets were quick to label Wolf as crippled for the remainder of his life, he appeared less eager to accept the idea of a handicapped parking placard dangling from the dog truck's rearview mirror. We, too, were not quick to throw in the towel, since many dogs in our kennel had received dire diagnoses over the years, yet went on to prove the veterinarians wrong.

I remember Cole and I wilted when a litter of pups came down with parvovirus and the veterinarian told us that, in all likelihood, none would survive. Still, we beat the odds and they pulled through. Despite no reported cases in the veterinary literature of Alaskan huskies having hip dysplasia, radiographs revealed one of our females suffered this genetically inherited ailment, but with diligence we provided her ample hip-friendly exercise and a satisfying quality of life as a house dog. For years people forewarned us that "wheezers" (dogs with laryngeal paralysis) couldn't be sled dogs, but we volunteered two of our wheezing wonders for an experimental throat-muscle "tie-back" surgery. Now, one of them annually pulls the sled thousands of miles with no ill effects, while the other—expected to die before her second birthday—recently turned thirteen, and while never displaying a penchant for pulling, she always kept up while accompanying us on thousands of miles of hiking, backpacking, and snowshoeing trips over those years.

Wolf was no exception. Like the proverbial phoenix, he rose from the ashes of his bleak prognosis, refusing to accept being anything less than a first-string runner. The road to his recovery was long, though. His original owner did his fair share of the work: teaching him to walk again, then run, then eventually to pull a sled. Wolf even participated in a local race and finished in good fashion, although this musher questioned if more racing would realistically be in his future.

Not long afterward, this fellow decided to move out of state. Before departing, he sold his entire kennel to an up-and-coming dog driver. However, the new owner had no interest in a question mark like Wolf, so we got a call inquiring if we'd add him to our kennel. As mushers who believed in giving dogs every chance to succeed, we accepted Wolf without hesitation.

It seemed more like destiny than a decision in some way, since we had been there the night of the accident, I had written several articles tracking his recovery for the local newspaper, and in general, we felt a vested interest in his well-being.

Wolf was wary of us and the other dogs at first. He leaned away from attempts to pet him, spent hours sulking in his box, and when plugged into the team for the first few runs he got nippy with dogs next to him. But with time and effort he quickly grew to accept us and join the pack. We didn't take him in hoping to add another A-team dog. We merely wanted to keep him happy and healthy. We decided we would only push him within the limits of his comfort, but our training techniques may have been the best thing for continuing to improve his condition.

Part of his successful recuperation resulted from the generous amount of exercise our dogs get through play. A husky's skills of retrieval may pale in comparison to a Labrador's, but we have found that many, if not most, of the dogs in our kennel love to fetch. We'll gather a pack of a dozen dogs at a time, then whip a rubber squeaky ball as far as we can across the yard. The dogs sprint 100-or-so yards to be the fastest and first to get it, and then lope back to us chasing whoever proudly has the prized possession clenched in their mandibles.

Wolf absolutely obsessed over this pastime, to such a degree that, I think, if given the choice between only being able to either mush or fetch until retirement, he would never put a harness on again and never look back at his decision. He loved fetching, and all the sprinting, stopping on a dime, jumping into the air to catch the ball, and whirling around to run back. It did wonders to build up his muscles and stretch his ligaments.

We also cross-train our dogs with plenty of paddling action by swimming them in a gin-clear pond not far from the kennel. The water never gets warm enough to be comfortable to most people, so with the exception of a few hardy souls and the occasional spindly legged shorebird, we have the entire area to ourselves most days. Cole and I wear wetsuits and alternate our laps to keep up with the dogs, spending entire evenings after work swimming them back and forth.

Physiologists studying sled dogs have figured out that one minute of swimming is equal to about four minutes of running. Using this formula and timing our swims, we deduced our dogs were getting the equivalent of a fifteen-mile run with every swim, every other day. We considered this not bad training for the "off-season," and it worked wonders for Wolf's strength and flexibility.

As the endlessly long days of summer eventually shortened and the brisk bite of autumn's onset began, we switched our training to the black sand beaches of Cook Inlet, less than a quarter mile from our kennel. In this scenic locale, eagles soared overhead on the thermals, while in the water sea otters and seals—curious about the rare spectacle of running dogs—periscoped up from the inlet's glassy surface for a better look, sometimes just yards away from where the team was trotting along the water's edge. Typically, the only tracks we encountered in the wet sand were the dogs own, or those left behind from the occasional bear foraging on the flotsam of fish scraps still lingering in the high-tide line. So overall,

Penny and Wolf lead Colleen's team while on a tour. No dog came as far, or demonstrated the truly indelible spirit of the sled dog, like Wolf did after having his leg shattered by a speeding car that collided with a team.

the atmosphere was mentally therapeutic for all parties involved, but the dogs also quickly became bulletproof strong from pulling a four-wheeler in this soft shoreline environment.

By the start of the winter race season, Wolf looked as good as any other dog in the kennel. The more miles we threw at him, the stronger he mentally and physically became. His first race with us was a 200-miler, the Gin Gin 200. While Cole took the best of the best for our kennel, I helmed the B-team, which included Wolf, and despite minus-forty-degree temperatures, tricky terrain on the icy rivers, and numerous steep climbs with blow-your-beard-off rapid descents down the far sides, Wolf never flinched in the face of these naturally occurring adversities. We finished in a respectable fifth place overall.

The following season, after another summer of fetching and swimming, Wolf's rehabilitation appeared complete, so Cole decided to add him to her A-team lineup in the toughest 200-mile event in the state, the Tustumena 200. This was going to be Wolf's litmus test.

The T-200 only has around six miles of flat trail; for the rest of the course teams are struggling to surmount the numerous mountain slopes. Cole intended to race to the fullest, rather than running to condition the dogs or to practice passing other teams as we occasionally sought to do when signing up for events. She would be, in car racing terms, putting the pedal to the metal.

She ended up coming in fourth, and Wolf was right there with her, actually leading the entire second half alongside our main race leader, Penny. They crossed the finish line looking eager to keep on going, and Cole earned the Humanitarian Award for her excellent care and conditioning of her team.

Back at the kennel, we watched Wolf closely for several days, and stretched his limbs to see if he was sore, but he showed no signs of having discomfort anywhere in his leg, ankle, or paw. He not only appeared as fit and healthy as any other member of the A-team, when the harnesses came out, he acted as enthusiastically about getting back on the trail as any of our race veterans. With the Iditarod looming only weeks away, we decided Wolf would make the cut for *the* team.

Cole went into the big race hoping to run an aggressive race schedule. In her rookie running, she had moved cautiously, as most first-timers do, to learn the route, terrain, and checkpoints. She finished thirty-sixth out of seventy-one mushers in her inaugural run, getting fourteen dogs to Nome and all of them looking exceptional. This time she wanted to use what she had learned to shave as many positions off her final placement as she could without compromising any of the dogs. We hoped Wolf could do the unbelievable and make it the whole 1,000-mile distance.

That season's Iditarod tested the entire team's toughness and tenacity as Mother Nature displayed her talents for manipulating the winter elements. Pitiless piles of snow several feet deep mired competitors' teams for the first half of the race that traverses the Alaska Range. These conditions were followed by huge ground blizzards howling across immense patches of treeless tundra in the state's interior section, and not even dogs' claws could get a grip on the wind-polished glare ice that plagued them once on the coast of the Bering Sea.

It's common in 1,000-mile races for some dogs to be dropped to veterinarians due to fatigue, illness, or ailment. In the safety and best interest of several dogs in her team, Cole sent a few home as they became sore or too tired.

Not Wolf.

He never fatigued or showed any signs of injury or poor health. He kept powerfully plugging along, leaning deep into his harness, nose to the ground, ceaselessly digging in with all fours to keep pulling forward.

The long miles alone with the dogs on the trail are always periods of deep introspection, and the bond between musher and dogs is never stronger than when relying on each other in the wild. Cole was particularly moved by Wolf's performance. Calling home from one of the checkpoints not far from the finish line, I remember her extolling for nearly the entire conversation his enduring resolve, and how inspiring his athleticism was to bear witness to.

In the last couple hundred miles, the real superstars—the most robust dogs—begin to shine. Cole relied on three leaders to get her to the end—the tireless Zoom, the pint-sized powerhouse Penny, and the dog who "would never run again," Wolf. As they crossed the finish line in Nome in twenty-first place in one of the most competitive fields seen in this event, he was still there, pulling in the swing position as hard as he had out of the starting chute in Anchorage, but now on the other side of the state.

In the human world, it's often said that our flaws give us character, and had a professional human athlete been struck by a car and then after healing and training gone on to finish a marathon, their achievement would be publicly admired, parents might consider them role models, news agencies would likely report of the greatness of this feat, and a few people might even hail them as a hero.

Wolf convinced me this same canon should hold true for sled dogs. He heroically overcame his adversities, largely due to his own strength of spirit, but also partially due to being given the opportunity, and this latter point should not be overlooked.

I understand—in some ways—how not every dog owner would take on the responsibility of a dog with a verified physical capacity of less than 100 percent. In fact, from our own experiences with some in the sport, I'm not sure how many mushers would have even forked over the cash for the surgery that saved Wolf's leg in the first place.

Allocating so much to mend one dog is difficult for those who have to weigh each and every financial expenditure against the sum total of savings they have on hand for the whole kennel. So, sometimes a good-of-the-many-outweighs-the-good-of-the-one logic prevails. Rather than risking—with no certainty of a successful outcome—several thousand dollars to mend a single dog, euthanasia is deemed the viable alternative.

This, I'm certain, has led to some of the skewed statistics in the veterinary literature in regard to sled dogs. How could the survivability numbers not be off, if dogs with parvovirus, hip dysplasia, laryngeal paralyses, or broken limbs are perpetually put down rather than receiving attempts at treatment for their injuries and ailments, and these efforts accurately recorded?

But beyond arguing the scientific merits, I'm a big believer that mushers should endeavor to make dogs well, purely for the virtuous reason of it being its own reward.

Sled dogs—at least the ones I've known—all shared the inherent qualities of having an undeterred spirit in the face of hardship and an overall resilience. These characteristics are not shocking, since they've been bred for them. They also excel at performing for mushers an array of feats as amazing as they are appalling. These dogs will—and do with some regularity in ultramarathons like the Iditarod—literally run themselves to death. They'll run until they're shitting streams of blood from the strain, until their stomachs ulcer from the stress, and until they aspirate—chocking to death—from vomiting food they didn't have time to completely digest before running the next leg of the race.

Knowing this, I've always been plagued by how any musher could ask an animal to bear the burden of so much for their own selfish reasons (psychological accomplishment, emotional enjoyment, financial gain, whatever) and then, in good conscience, not make *every* effort to repay those sacrifices.

It's frankly disgusting to me, and why when watching Wolf cross under the burled arch that marks the end of the Iditarod, I immediately grew maudlin by the seen and unseen in his performance. I, like the other fans crowding the finishing chute, cheered for the valuable contributions he made to the team that allowed for them all to make the final run up Front Street. But, unlike the throngs of fans who didn't know Wolf personally, I also felt a sentimental stirring of emotions at the thought of all this dog had overcome to earn the prestigious title of "Iditarod finisher."

In some ways, Wolf could teach us a lot about how to be better humans. He was a tough dog for sure—if he had been any tougher, he'd have rusted—but this was not his crowning attribute. He went above and beyond simply being steely.

Wolf had moxie. He embodied never giving up and never giving in, and my only sadness when thinking about his achievements is wondering how many other dogs with spirit like him are out there, or were out there, but never got the chance to prove themselves because their owners didn't have the same resolve.

What the Raven Showed Me

THE AIR HUNG HEAVY WITH THE PLACID SCENT OF FRESH SPRUCE as soft snow sifted from the low clouds, powdering the dogs' backs and tickling my cheeks with flakes as delicate as the fluttering of a moth's wings. Lulled by the rhythm of the run, I almost didn't notice the raven overhead. Against the featureless pewter-colored sky, the ebony bird was a distinctly dark contrast, but its behavior was what really commanded my attention.

Pacing my leaders, the raven craned its little head to peer earthward. It appeared mesmerized and flew with us for nearly a mile, but before it departed the raven pulled in one wing and did an aerial roll, flipping upside down for several seconds. Rather than tumbling out of the sky, it seemed to briefly defy gravity, then righted itself and picked up speed.

Which is it? I thought, remembering timeworn beliefs of Alaska Natives that a raven flies upside down to dump luck off its back or to shepherd humans in the direction of other animals.

I was mushing in the Skilak Wildlife Recreation Area, where a nineteen-mile road bisects the heavily wooded heart of the much larger Kenai National Wildlife Refuge, a 1.92-million-acre wilderness that serves as home to a wealth of wildlife. In summer the Skilak area is inundated with camera-clad tourists in their cars hoping to spot black and brown bears, which are quite common and confident in showing themselves since hunting in this neck of the woods is restricted to nothing larger than grouse and snowshoe hares.

In winter, however, after the lumbering RVs filled with summer folks have—like the ducks and geese—all fled south for the season and the bears have tucked themselves into their dens, the road goes unplowed and largely unused. I have often run the team from end to end in the exquisite emptiness, gliding for hours on the wide white ribbon without seeing any signs of human life, but an abundance of other rarely sighted fauna.

Mottled-gray spruce grouse and snowshoe hare with their large furry feet are the most common creatures I encounter. They're drawn to the different vegetation that grows in the openness and abundant sunlight along the edge of the forest. Unlike the shady struggle that plants endure under the thick stands of spruce trees that dominate this area, along the roadway willow bushes flourish—crowding each other in fact—and drawing herbivores to their succulent shoots and buds. Larger predators follow.

Lynx, with their heavily padded paws, flared facial fur, and tufts of black on their ear tips, are quite common, and I've seen a few adult cats as large as Labradors over the years. They utilize the roadside to their advantage, standing motionless in the tangled, leafless mesh of willow while waiting to get a glimpse of their quarry. It is both a good offense and defense for lynx, since the camouflage of their frost-colored coat blends in perfectly.

I've crossed paths with quite a few coyotes too—sharp-nosed, slightly smaller and more slender-built carnivore cousins to my own pack. They also know the comings and goings of wild birds and bunnies, and are remarkable at catching rodents, although coyotes tend to be fleeter of foot than lynx upon realizing they've been spotted.

This day, though, the raven hinted at another species. There are numerous rolling hills along Skilak, where pockets of bone-chilling air always settle in the low points, making each rise an acute pleasure. Two-thirds of the way into the run, I crested the top of one particularly lofty point, and spied a four-legged figure in the distance.

There, sniffing something in the middle of the hard-packed surface of the icy road, stood an inconceivably large, lone canine. Whatever its nose had drawn it to captured its full attention. It stood broadside to us, revealing its immensity—the thick neck stretched out, big head held low, and sensuously sculpted snout doing its highly developed olfactory duty.

Wolf! I thought.

The creature's stocky stature was intimidating, even at a distance. Hard looking and lean, as befitting an animal living in the wilds of Alaska. All four limbs were lithe and longer than even my most stilt-legged dogs, and its grayish-brown coat was thicker than the coats of any member of my pack, particularly around the neck and shoulders where the fur turned mane-like.

Like glimpsing an apparition, I became spellbound by the sighting of this animal that until that moment had been eternally elusive. It felt like electricity flowed through my body as every neuron in my brain must have fired at once. Deep in my chest, the ventricles of my heart fluttered. The hair on my neck rose. I knew what I saw standing before me, but still couldn't quite believe my own perception. The creature seemed larger than life, far surpassing the mental imagery of what a wolf could and would look like, particularly when compared to the handful of others I've seen in captivity over the years.

My thoughts flashed back to boyhood and the first wolves I ever saw, in a zoo, in the days before planners attempted to create enclosures with the aesthetics of a natural habitat. There were two—a sad fate in itself for pack animals—in a tiny, probably ten-by-ten-foot cage with iron bars, and nothing for them to lie on but a cold, concrete slab. They both looked completely broken. One lay listless while the other looked through us as if we didn't exist and paced, feverishly, longing to be elsewhere—not really a surprise for those who know a wild wolf pack may roam across hundreds of acres.

I remember feeling sorry for those wolves. I wondered how long it had been since they had truly run. I worried if they still remembered the wild—moving through thick stands of fir trees, the feel of soft moss beneath their pads, the sound of prey snapping a twig nearby, and the scent of a wild vole, ptarmigan, or larger quarry—and if they did recall this past life, did it make their present internment better or worse.

While one may argue that no animals should be in captivity—since after all, saving wild creatures does little good if we don't save the wild habitats they hail from—with wolves captivity seems an atrocious indignity. Few beings represent the spirit of the wilderness the way wolves do, which is why they have become such an iconic symbol—from the ancient, oral traditions of Native cultures to the modern animal-rights movement. In many national parks they have become the poster animal for the American outdoor experience, and here in Alaska, hundreds of thousands of tourists flock to Denali National Park annually hoping for a glimpse of one of these wild canines. There you at least stand a chance of spotting one, but closer to our kennel, the odds are much lower, which was part of what made this Skilak sighting so spectacular.

At one time the Kenai Peninsula boasted one of the largest species of wolves in North America, *Canis lupus alces*. It was said to measure five to seven feet in length, from its nose to the tip of its tail, stand just shy of four feet tall at the shoulder (only a few inches shorter than African lions), and weigh in at a whopping 150 to 200 pounds. As its scientific name implies, this wolf was adapted to hunting moose (*Alces alces*).

Unfortunately, as is often the case when humans and wolves begin to intermingle, it is man who shows his vicious side. By 1915, after years of poisoning and trapping, this wolf species was extirpated by gold miners that swept into the area. Roughly fifty years later, wolves began emigrating back down to the peninsula from the northern interior of Alaska, but from a different and smaller subspecies, only tipping the scales to around 85 to 115 pounds. While no recent population estimates have been done, wildlife managers generally believe there are between 100 and 200 wolves currently on the peninsula.

Not all are ecstatic about their return. Few creatures inspire the imagination to swirl, prompt as much heated discussion, or cause such visceral reaction for saving or taking the life of an animal, as much as wolves. In Alaska—one of the last strongholds of their population—wolves are frequently maligned by the hunting fraternity, snared by trappers on land, and aerially shot from small planes.

This treatment of wolves cuts to the marrow of the attitude the cavalier have toward them. Rather than inspiring respect from humans, this member of the canid family is regarded as something to be feared, controlled, and eventually conquered. This is why the wolf—wild, untamable, and a symbol of uncontrollable nature—is so easily and readily made into a target, particularly by those who hunt the same big game animals for sport that the wolves hunt for food.

Despite the fact that wolves have coexisted for millennia without hunting to extinction the hoofed animals they prey on, a large swath of society surmises that these carnivores—simply by existing—threaten moose and numerous other "game" species with utter annihilation. I've met these folks firsthand while reporting for various newspapers; the first sobering and equally nauseating experience came while covering a meeting held by the local trappers association. I had never been in a room with so many people filled with rage against rather than reverence for wolves, but still one among them stood out as particularly sadistic.

He had a burly build and an unkempt appearance, complete with scraggly hair and beard, and equal measures of dirt and dried blood on his coveralls. He reminded me of a wild boar more than a man, and once he began boasting I became convinced he lacked the emotional qualities that define the latter. With perverse pleasure, he detailed the dispatching of the last hapless wolf he had lured into one of his neck snares. Unlike some that are immediately choked to death by the cinching noose of cable, this poor animal was still alive when he came upon it.

The boar explained how the wolf was a "ferocious fighter," clear to read from the obvious signs in the snow, where it had clawed and pawed for hours in what must have been desperate attempts to escape. He was proud of how much the poor creature suffered, and indifferent that he was the cause of that suffering.

"So what'd ya use to put it down, a .22?" inquired another trapper.

"Nah, why waste a bullet and put a hole in the pelt," bragged the boar. "I carry a two by four and crack 'em over the head. Not too hard, but enough to stun 'em, then I put my boot over their throat and keep it there till they're dead."

Having elaborated the blow-by-blow of his execution method, he beamed with pride in a way that would make anyone other than sociopaths shudder.

Thankfully, not everyone loathes wolves. Some people are equally passionate about protecting them, myself included, partially from a life spent with forty dogs. While I, like most wolf biologists, don't know as much as we would like about wild wolves due to their elusive behavior, I do know that their family bonds are built with industrial-strength glue. They will ferociously defend their family members and their home range from interlopers. New members from outside the family group are taken in very slowly and only after paying their dues at the periphery of the pack for extended periods of time. Pups are often cared for by the entire family —including the father, somewhat rare in the animal world—and by six months old may begin traveling long distances and hunting with the pack.

We have seen these same parallels in our kennel. Once the dogs became established as a cohesive group, they grew close-knit with one another, whether while running in a team or living their daily routines within the kennel. Loose dogs—Shagoo being the most diligent—vehemently patrolled the borders and did not welcome intruders of any kind: wild animals, other dogs, or even humans that weren't familiar. Related kin not only got along better when housed next to each other or paired to run side-by-side in the team, but these family units also defended each other when occasional squabbles broke out. Mothers would join the fray or form grudges with dogs that had fought with her adult offspring, as would brothers and sisters who were present when a sibling had a skirmish.

Also, like wild wolves, pups—my daughter included—were more eagerly accepted by the group than young or adult dogs from the pound or elsewhere. Those born on the property would play with nearly all the dogs when loose, at around six months old they also began running along with teams being conditioned, and by a year old were in harness training alongside adult racers for short runs. Once fully fledged as a member of the pack, any separation felt sorrowful. Since not all forty dogs can run at any one time, those left behind howl mournfully, just like wolves at the den anxiously awaiting pack members to return from a hunt.

Human and dogs alike, covered in ice and snow, on a training run in minus temperatures. In these far-flung locales, where the only audible utterances of life were the soft panting of husky breath and the voices in our own heads, we were in our element.

Compared to puppies born into the kennel, dogs from the pound also took more time to introduce to the pack. Like wild wolves, we would initially stake newcomers to the outside of the communal area rather than attempting to integrate them into a position in the center. Also, with activities such as feeding, brushing, and fetching, we adhered to the standards set by wild canines—that newcomers have to start out as the low animal in the overall hierarchy to keep the peace, and while we spoiled the additions so they'd feel at home, we made sure not to favor them *before* the others.

Over the years we became more than a disjointed accumulation of humans and dogs. Cole, Lynx, and I, and all the dogs, became a connected unit, a kindred pack, and caring family. When we moved across the land, we did so together and dependent on each other. We moved as one in a way that can't be understood by those who travel to the same area we do, but by snowmachine. Stepping on a dog team transports us not only to a time before man relied on mechanization, but even further back, to a time when man and wolf existed together and commingled to start down the long path that—we don't know *how*, but we know *did*—lead to the domestic dog.

Perhaps it was this relationship with my dogs, and our subsequent attachment to the wilderness we shared together, that caused such a swelling of sentimental emotions when I did see the wild wolf firsthand and on its own terms. The sighting immediately made clear why this wild canine's reputation has been so enduring and how some are galvanized to stand up for this species' right to exist. Sharing the same space with this wolf moved me deeply. I noticed an immediate euphoric tingle, as though my soul quivered. I had to remind myself to breathe.

Even in Denali, most of my wolf sightings happened from a bus full of tourists, but I was glimpsing this one by myself. It felt like nature was sharing a secret with me alone. Everything else fell away from my perception and time seemed at a standstill.

But it wasn't.

My domestic pack was pressing closer and closer with each passing second. The wolf had no idea of our existence. Unlike snowmachines, which give off a two-stroke stench and emit an insect-like whine that can be heard miles away, dog teams make almost no noise while on the move.

Aside from the soft swish of the sled across the snow and light panting of the dogs' breath, the team is silent, which—for good and bad—can make it almost too easy to sneak up on wild animals.

The dogs, having seen the wolf when I did, were really driving hard to get up to it, their front and back paws meeting in midair. It wasn't until we were roughly a team's length, maybe sixty to seventy feet, from the wolf that it registered our presence and close proximity. Still not entirely back from the trance of wonder the wolf sighting shrouded me in, the thought of stepping on the brake hadn't even dawned on me, but luckily one of the dogs in the team let out a yelp of excitement as we were closing in.

The wolf, which easily dwarfed even my largest dog by thirty pounds, jerked to attention. Its head and ears snapped in our direction. Caught off guard, it startled at seeing a pack of its not-so-distant kin so close, and with their radars locked on target. In one soundless bound the wolf leapt off the road and disappeared into the trees as though it truly were a specter.

Its retreat was so swift, had I blinked I would have missed it. The hasty withdrawal also illustrated a belief I hold dear: that far from being murderous marauders, wolves are almost always more scared of us than we are of them.

I savored what I had seen, replaying it instantly in my mind's eye, hoping to burn the ember of the wolf's image deep into the log of my memory. On the Yukon Quest and Iditarod, Cole witnessed wolves, foxes, and once even a wolverine emerge to lope along with the team, but to this day, Skilak is the only place I've seen a wild wolf while running dogs.

For the remainder of the journey my thoughts were filled not only with the grandeur of the wolf, but also that of raven. I mulled over the relationship between these intelligent birds and wolves. While this experience represented my first actual wolf sighting, I had for years traveled in their wake. Mushing in remote areas where the land seemed too stark to serve as any animal's territory and the constant cold typically served as my only companion besides the dogs, astonishingly from time to time, I've seen paw prints of wolves—twice the size of my largest dog—etched into the smooth, sinuous contours of the frozen landscape. On other occasions I've passed

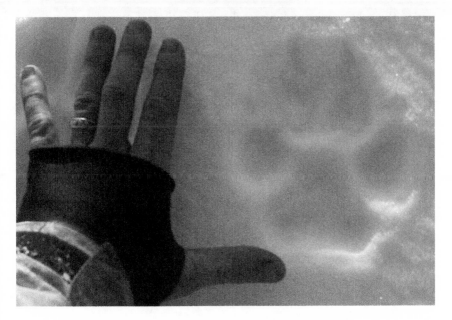

My hand next to the paw print of a wild wolf.

the remnants of kill sites where a pack had dragged down a moose, and scarcely any parts remained from these massive ungulates except the gnawed-on long bones, spine, and the ribcage where ravens now perched and pecked for any morsels of meat the carnivores left behind.

In recent years, several biologists, and the Inuit, Yup'ik, and Iñupiat Eskimos before them, have suggested that perhaps wolves learn from the behavior of ravens where game might be. By watching for wing dips or possibly even being deliberately called by the croaking birds, wolves will upon arrival open up a downed animal's body cavity, making eating easier for the talon-lacking, blunt-billed birds to gain sustenance.

I also recalled another myth traditionally held by many Alaska Natives, and began perseverating on it—the idea that prior to people and animals being fixed in our current physical forms, we used to be able to *talk* to each other. My experience left me with the notion that maybe sometimes they still do, but only a few humans have the uncanny ability to notice the subtle signs and comprehend the ethereal messages being conveyed to us.

I'm not claiming to be a Dr. Doolittle, but on more than one occasion I did get the sense an animal was trying to tell me something important. I've experienced lead dogs that had listened to voice directions for years suddenly not obey a forward command, and only moments later, after falling through thin ice, realizing they were trying to warn me of what lurked ahead. While hiking in summer, I could swear magpies and Canadian jays have signaled to me with their shrieking, then gone a few yards farther up the trail to find a moose carcass encircled by fresh bear tracks.

And on this day, I definitely felt like the raven—encountered in a remoteness where animals still own the land more than humans, and where nature often gives gifts to those willing to spend uncountable hours in its splendor—had bestowed on me one of many rewards for living with the land, not against it. After years of longing to see a wild wolf, the raven granted my wish and for that gift I am—and forever will be—grateful.

Rescue You, Rescue Me

I N ADDITION TO THE WAFTING FETOR THAT ASSAULTED MY olfactory system, unmistakably feces and lots of it, the air was also thick with the scent of canine hopelessness. The emaciated dogs didn't have much more left in them. They looked cadaverous, every one of them, like living skeletons with only a thin layer of skin stretched over their bones. Some were so skinny, with stomachs so concave, and bodies so wholly retracted—they looked as if literally trying to digest themselves.

Yet, somehow, a few of the friendlier ones mustered the strength to weakly wag their tails at the sight of us. My vision became a watery blur, and I had to pinch the bridge of my nose to stop the tears that welled up at the thought of these dogs showing any emotion besides depths of disgust for human beings. They would have been justified based on their lives up to that point.

Not all the survivors were so inclined to be forgiving. Poorly socialized, even when they were "cared" for, they wanted no part of us strangers, and cowered or did their best to scuttle away and hide in whatever dilapidated structure they were using for shelter. None had doghouses in the traditional sense of the word. Instead, most were chained up under spindly trees, while a few were tethered to a blackened, burned-out car chassis, and still others were hitched to whatever piece of garbage had been left behind and lay near enough to crawl under and get partially out of the elements.

A canine concentration camp.

That was the most accurate way to describe the appearance of the abandoned kennel and it was my first impression of the situation that led to Ibn—a floppy-eared, black-and-tan-colored dog that looked like he had as much Rhodesian ridgeback in him as husky—joining our kennel. It is a tale that illustrates the worst of human character as much as it does the best of a dog's nature.

Breakup—that late-winter to early-spring time of year when the weather can't decide how miserable it wants to make northern dwellers—was peaking. The ground remained frozen and rock hard, but the longer days and burgeoning warmth had triggered a season's worth of snow to melt, causing great lakes of standing water to pool everywhere. Clearly, at least a week or two of more sunshine would be required for the ground to thaw enough to soak the slurry up.

The annual deluge is always a challenging time for mushers, and most responsible folks will, in fall, bring in fill or take other measures to build their dog yards up to a slightly higher elevation than the surrounding area. In our own yard we also carve and maintain drain channels to divert melting snow and water away from the dogs.

Ibn, along with his kennelmates, was not so lucky and experiencing the brunt of sloppy, between-the-seasons weather. They had all been abandoned by their owner, which led to me being present at the scene. The Alaska State Troopers hailed a private animal-rescue facility to liberate the dozen or so dogs, and the owner of the rescue facility called me—working as a newspaper journalist at the time—to document the appalling environmental conditions as well as the rescue efforts, in case the matter ended up in court after animal-neglect charges were filed.

As relayed to me, the dogs belonged to a sixteen-year-old girl and wannabe musher who had become pregnant. After splitting up with her live-in boyfriend of roughly the same age, the girl decided to move three hours away to be closer to her mother. She said she left the dogs in her ex-boyfriend's care. The ex-boyfriend said no such arrangement was ever made. It was a classic "he said, she said," with the dogs caught in the middle and suffering.

For days that turned into weeks, the dogs survived with little care or food. The only thing that kept them alive at all was the compassion of a few neighbors. Most Alaskans loathe all forms of authority and have a strong mentality of "to each their own," so neighbors that on a daily basis drove past the dogs, initially, didn't want to get the law involved. But eventually, some folks must have decided they couldn't sit back and watch the poor animals starve to death.

They at first intervened by occasionally scattering a few scoops of dry dog food, but after a couple weeks of waiting for the dogs' owners to return, and growing weary of watching the dogs scavenge on a smattering of kibble, one neighbor finally had enough and called the troopers to report the situation.

The moment I stepped from my truck, just based on the nauseating smell, I thought there had to be dead, decaying dogs somewhere on-site, and the more I saw, the more I was sure had the troopers been called just a day or two later, there would have been.

Ibn, as we later named him (none of the dogs at the scene had names anyone knew) immediately caught my eye. He had what, a few weeks earlier, was probably the best shelter during the cold of winter—a large ten-hole dog box typically seen on the bed of a pickup truck, and used to haul dogs to and from races and other places. Ditched on the ground with the dog box doors open and breakup in full swing, the cubbyholes were now flooded, and not just with water.

Since the chained dogs had been neglected for weeks to possibly months, their personal areas were a sty, filled with sickeningly sloppy mounds of feces easily measuring knee-deep on the dogs. Stool mixed with the melting snow, polluting the puddles and turning them into nothing short of putrid cesspools that the hapless creatures had to stand in day in and day out, and were forced to drink from as their sole water source. The grisliness of the scene stabbed at me, but I was thankful it hadn't been any later in the year, when warm enough for flies to be out. The problem of unchecked poop piles would have become compounded by a frenzy of maggots boiling out of the decaying excreta, as we have witnessed during eerily similar summer rescues.

Saving sled dogs put Cole and me on the front lines of these kinds of tragic scenarios far too often for two people who love dogs. In Alaska, the animal abuse laws are extremely antiquated. Due to terminology that the abuse or neglect to dogs must be done purposefully with the intent of causing harm or suffering, few people get charged for the suffering of animals at their hands. We've seen many cases where people who had abandoned dogs simply said, "I never meant to harm them," "I just got in over my head," or "I ran out of money," and they got off with minimal legal repercussions. And these were just the people whose despicable deeds made it onto the radar of the authorities.

Outside the city limits, there are no animal control entities in our part, and most parts, of Alaska. Culling runs rampant, including—albeit secretly—in many kennels in the mushing community. It's a hush-hush thing with outsiders of the sport, this silence learned after mushers in the past who openly spoke about or wrote books discussing culling felt the backlash from animal rights organizations and pet-loving fans, or suffered losses of financial backing from already squeamish sponsors.

When we were at our peak of mushing, and considered "just like them" by people who didn't realize our differing animal ethics, it was amazing to me how many professional mushers would openly talk to us about dogs they killed for being too slow, having a bad gait, being picky eaters, and myriad other subjective criteria. The old "shoot, shovel, and shut up," as it is colloquially known.

Once people realized we were "sensitive types," we heard less of this kind of talk, but then we got approached by their handlers—people hired seasonally in the bigger operations to train and clean up after the dogs. Initially not knowing about the dark underbelly of the sport, these handlers would tell us about the dogs that were being killed by the mushers they worked for, and plead with us to stop it in some way or direct them to authorities that could. This caused rifts between us and some of these other mushers with differing ideologies about the inherent worth of a dog's life.

Ibn—a floppy-eared, black-and-tan-colored dog—joined our kennel after being rescued from deplorable conditions. When we found him, he had spent weeks suffering in the equivalent of a canine concentration camp.

I know it's hard to believe any musher could be so inhumane, and I understand why fans are incredulous that some of the heroes they admire and idolize could ever commit these horrible atrocities. I suffered this naivety myself in the beginning.

I never expect those guilty of these atrocities to admit them, and I would hate to imply that all mushers kill dogs, because that's not the case. Not the case at all. But, it is a sad truth, and an ugly truth, that over the years we have known people who killed or abandoned canines that were perfectly healthy, their dogs' only flaw being an inability to meet some arbitrary performance standard. I only bring it up in this context because until people know about these abominable actions, situations like Ibn's will continue to take place, and dogs—*all* dogs, as intelligent, sentient, loving beings—deserve better.

Ibn's only refuge from the swamped stockade that had come to be his home was to stand, sleep, and basically live on the roof of the box. A survivor, deserted on an island, surrounded by a sea of shit. Living on top offered Ibn only minimal respite though.

He had no refuge from the sleet and rain that had fallen since his abandonment, no ability to dry off when it stopped precipitating, and no straw bed under him for insulation during the still-freezing night temperatures. These would be tough conditions for any dog to shiver through, but it must have been unbearably punishing for Ibn and these dogs since they hadn't taken in adequate calories for who knew how long.

Ibn and the others were rounded up and brought back to the rescue facility to start the long road to physical and mental recovery. My part of the story was done so I headed back to the office and eventually home, but I couldn't stop thinking about the horrors I observed and that those poor creatures had lived through. At the dinner table, standing in the shower, lying awake in bed for hours—I couldn't get the images I had seen out of my mind. Over the next few days I checked on the dogs repeatedly.

A bittersweet trend I've noticed with animal rescue stories, and perhaps a hallmark of the cult of celebrity that dominates much of America, is that the same suffering dogs that many people would have been completely indifferent to days before become highly sought-out for adoption after getting on the evening news or making the headlines of the local paper. Several of the dogs had already received new homes, but Ibn was still there, despite gaining weight quickly and still fairly happy in the face of the hardships he endured.

I drove out to see the ones not yet adopted and without realizing why, I gravitated toward Ibn. As I approached his new and much-improved quarters—a large, clean doghouse bursting with easily a half bale of straw that smelled as sweet as it was golden and fluffy—I didn't know what to expect. I drew near his small world slowly and respectfully.

Warmly snuggled in, he saw me and came out of his doghouse, cautiously at first, but almost immediately his tail wagged in happy little swishes. As dogs that are soliciting affection often do, he slid his nose under my hand until my palm was on the top of his head. I looked into his chocolate-brown eyes and in that moment knew he had to come home with me.

Back at our kennel, we initially had no name for him, but the dog soon-to-be-known-as Ibn quickly took to Cole and me, and was friendly with all the other dogs, even the other males. He fit in well with one exception: he was a *prolific* digger—quite possibly a stereotype that developed as a way to self-stimulate when he got bored during his neglected period.

It didn't matter how hard or coarse the substrate, once Ibn set his mind and paws to excavating, he didn't stop. He burrowed with the zeal of an archaeologist on the verge of a new fossil find. It became a common sight to see Ibn at the bottom of a crater several feet deep, the tip of his tail sticking out, and pawfuls of sand flying through the air as he worked his way to the planet's core.

Aside from the eyesore it created, once the sun went down it become tough to see safe footing when feeding or checking on him. On more than one occasion while feeding at dusk, I misjudged a step, stumbled into one of his holes, and found myself a soggy mess after getting showered in a five-gallon bucket of soaked-out kibble. One such incident, not long after we acquired our digger, provided the inspiration for his name.

At the time, I was reading the Michael Crichton novel *Eaters of the Dead,* which is based loosely on the manuscript of Ahmad Ibn Fadlan's that related his experiences with Norsemen in A.D. 922. As he explains his long name (based on patriarchal lineage) to the Vikings, they pick up on the repetition of "Ibn," which meant "son of" in his Arabic tongue, so this is what they called him.

Since "Son of a . . ." became the mantra I exclaimed after unexpectedly vanishing into one of this dog's trenches, "Ibn" seemed like the perfect name for the newcomer.

It took Ibn a few years to get healthy and strong enough to train and race with the rest of the kennel. Weight can be put on quickly, but muscle takes a bit longer, and the muscular maturity to be able to run for hundreds of miles takes even longer still. Ibn was raring to go after about two years in our kennel. Cole raced him in several mid-distance events with the culmination of his racing career being a tenth-place finish in a running of the Tustumena 200—a raced hailed by many as the toughest 200-mile race in Alaska.

Ibn always pulled and could even be counted on to lead for short stints when Cole needed to give her main lead dogs a bit of a break, but he wasn't the fastest dog in the team, nor the strongest. As such, when I think back on Ibn, it was not his performance in the team that makes him stand out in my memory; it was his unique personality that made him so special.

Like a lump of coal put under immense pressure, Ibn came out of his abhorrent ordeal a diamond. He survived, undeniably changed—at least in terms of his understanding of humans, but still his personality remained, happy and whole, inside and out.

Ibn's true self showed through late one summer night. Cole and I were bushed after a long day of labor in the dog yard. We had been building and painting doghouses, filling holes dug by some of the dogs (no need to mention any names), and cooking up a fifty-gallon drum of white rice and whole-bodied sockeye salmon to give the dogs for dinner. Great white plumes of fish-scented smoke billowed up and floated off with the soft breeze. At dusk, we covered the makeshift cauldron to let it cool overnight and to contain the smell of the cooked fare from wafting too far from home, but apparently it didn't work.

Around 2 A.M. the dog yard erupted in a cacophony of excited barks. As a kennel owner, you not only learn to distinguish each dog's individual and distinct voice from the others, but you also perceive that the dogs as a whole emit different decibel calibers of barking. Wanting to be fed is one sound, a loose dog is another, and someone pulling up the driveway is equally distinct. The calamity of hysterical alarm barks they woke us with was their sound for "Intruder!" or something strange entering the yard, which typically meant an escaped dog wandering in from a neighboring kennel or a moose looking for a late night snack (since they loved to munch the willow that grew near the periphery of our dog yard).

From the loft of our tiny cabin, I groggily squinted out the book-sized window, looking in the direction the dogs were staring. Still in summer, a bit of rose-colored light loomed on the horizon, but being early in the morning the dim light made it impossible to identify exactly what kind of creature was prowling around our property. I could see something brown moving through the undulating sea of green, chest-high grass behind the dog yard. Based on the color and height—just a little less than the grass itself—I thought it must be a yearling moose.

Adult ungulates are more savvy at navigating their way around the dog yard, but from other firsthand encounters with inexperienced youngsters meandering in, I knew that if they became panicked, mama moose would quickly come to the rescue by stomping and kicking at any nearby dogs. Fearing for their safety, I launched out of bed in my underwear and sprinted outside clapping and yelling, "Go on now, you! Go on and get outta here!"

Halfway through the dog yard, a barrel-sized brown blur burst from the tall grass heading in my direction, and for good and bad there were half a dozen dogs between me and it. The dogs and I all realized at about the same time that the animal was not a moose, but a charging subadult grizzly, and with this sudden awareness all of the dogs but one dove into their doghouses.

Despite the bear being close enough for me to be engulfed by its musky, wild smell, I stood motionless. My entire system flooded with adrenaline and panic, all external concentration on the bruin, all internal concentration on not evacuating my bowels. Were it not for the detonation of raucous barking in the dog yard, I'm positive in that moment the bear could have heard my own heart thrashing the inside of my ribcage.

The bear's mass hulked, its shaggy coat bristled, its expression clearly one of surprise—which more often than not means danger. Yet Ibn, between the bear and me, remained out of his box, in an act as brave as it was ferocious. In a fury, he snapped his jaws in the air and savagely snarled, basically giving the bruin one hell of a hard time.

Ibn's blood boiled and his spirited show distracted the bear. The beast turned its attention from me to him and rushed at Ibn, but then paused, standing just out of his bite zone. From there the bruin took swipes with paws the size of Ibn's head. Young bears, lacking the confidence that will come with a few more years and a couple hundred more pounds, often threaten like this, without getting close enough to get hurt or bit themselves.

After a few seconds of this, and clearly outnumbered by a wide-eyed, two-legged underwear man and the hellhound determined to protect him, the bear turned tail and ran. While I froze catatonically except for quaking in my boxers, Ibn had stood his ground, and amazingly—and luckily—prevailed.

Speechless, and overcome by emotions ranging from gratitude, to awe, to envy, I dropped to my knees, letting them settle into the same sand where plate-sized paw prints from the bear left divots in the soft earth. With both hands, I affectionately scratched the loose skin of Ibn's neck for a while, a long while. He responded by leaning in, raising his nose to the air, and shifting his weight slightly to focus my fingers where he wanted them while still vigilantly peering over my shoulder.

The bear never returned and I've never forgotten that night. It's tough to say for certain whether it was karma that a dog I saved had in turn saved me, or if Ibn was just being territorial and defending his home and pack. Either way, Ibn displayed a courage the likes of which I have only seen a handful of times while actually owning, training, and racing dogs.

His actions reinforced to me merit can't always be weighed in terms of pulling performance. Not all dogs may end up being race champions due to their athletic ability, or lack thereof, but it doesn't mean they don't have worth, as individuals and on their own terms. *Every* dog's life matters, and as Ibn proved, even a dog given up on and left for dead, may still have beating within its chest the heart of a hero.

Dog Truck Dilemma

THE SUDDEN SILENCE WAS DEAFENING. THAT WAS MY FIRST thought, sitting in my broken-down dog truck, in the middle of nowhere, in minus forty temperatures, with four dogs riding shotgun. Moments before, everything was going well, but now, not a single thing inside the truck worked. It wouldn't run, wouldn't even start, and that meant no way to get the heater going to keep all of us warm, and possibly alive.

To be honest, the whole race had been a shit show from the beginning. It was Cole's fourth time competing in the Copper Basin 300 Sled Dog Race, a notoriously grueling event hailed by many as a mini-Iditarod due to the heavy doses of reality it can dispense to the pseudo-tough or woefully unprepared.

Located in the Copper Basin region, essentially a bowl between four mountain ranges—the Chugach, the Wrangell-St. Elias, the Talkeetna, and the Alaska Range—the topography creates a high-pressure zone that presses and pools frigid air into a low spot, making it an icebox with temperatures seemingly cold enough to freeze the blood in your veins. The CB300 also possesses numerous rugged mountain climbs, including the highest peak of any sled dog race in the state. Deep drifts of snow between checkpoints, some with accumulations more than a foot over the height of the dogs' backs, are standard fare.

River ice frequently freezes so solid, thick, and heavy that it presses down on the still liquid water below, the pressure forcing it to squeeze up in liquid form. This "overflow" is indistinguishable from the hard, smooth glaze beneath it until dogs and musher splash through it, having their boots and booties instantly encased in ice. These sections of overflow, like death and taxes, are certainties, particularly on the wide Gakona River and the fast-flowing Excelsior Creek, which never seems to solidify no matter how low the mercury drops.

In spite of, and because of, all these challenges, Cole always favored the race. She saw each and every running as a test of all her mushing skills. It brought to the surface a sea of self-doubts to quell and conquer, exposed chinks in the armor of her winter wardrobe and layering system that she immediately fixed upon returning home, and it showed her any over-looked aspects of our training program that she would further fine-tune with the remainder of the racing season. Crossing the finish line annually didn't just mean an end to the race; for her it meant another personal and substantial victory.

Getting to the race is roughly a ten-hour drive from our kennel, depending on the winter driving conditions (slab avalanches closing the road are common) and how many breaks we take to drop the dogs (usually every three hours). Once on the race trail, the mushers travel a loop 300 miles long, and their support crews—which for Cole was me— always drive an equal distance with a tenth of the rest. This inconvenience is due to the scant amount of roads connecting the checkpoint lodges, bars, and campgrounds. The path we the handlers have to travel is a clover pattern, rather than a circle, with the dog truck having to make the long trek up and back each leaf of the clover.

The CB300 alternated the starting point and direction each year, and for our kennel's fourth attempt, the race began in Paxson. We arrived, checked in, did all our evening chores, and turned in early hoping to get plenty of rest. We knew we'd both likely sleep less than eight cumulative hours over the next three days—Cole due to racing and tending to the dogs when not on the trail, me due to driving and staying awake at checkpoints with Cole to keep her morale up as a fugue state from sleep deprivation inevitably set in.

Our alarm woke us at midnight, set so we could throw on some warm clothes, wander outside, and drop the dogs to relieve themselves at least once during the night. Any grogginess we felt instantly wore off as we stepped into the negative temperatures.

I also immediately felt my cold lips crack, the result of grimacing at a gaseous spectacle that greeted us. During the night another musher pulled in next to our dog truck, and apparently had forgotten to bring an extension cord to plug his truck in to keep critical engine components warm when not running. Instead, this dullard had left his truck idling and with a zephyr blowing in the direction of our truck, all the noxious exhaust fumes were flowing right into our dog boxes. In the worst-case scenario this could have asphyxiated our dogs, and at the very least it would have made them sick as hell right before an extremely arduous test of their cardiovascular and respiratory stamina.

We had no way of knowing whose truck it was or how long the gassing had been going on, so we expeditiously checked on our dogs. Seeing they were alive and alert, we moved the truck posthaste. One of the only spots still available was next to a dog truck I knew belonged to Rick Swenson—the only five-time Iditarod champion in history. His truck was plugged into his own portable generator/battery charger rather than into an outlet of the inn like everyone else's. With generator-envy rather than an actual one, we outstretched numerous extension cords we had brought along, snaking them to the outlet we had already been using.

The next day the trouble continued. During the drawing for starting positions, Cole drew forty-first out of fifty-one mushers. Going out this far back in the pack is always less than ideal because not only will front-running teams often break out any thin ice bridges that exist over streams and rivers, but the overall condition of the trail itself degrades with every passing team due to the paws of each twelve-dog string churning up and softening the once-packed trail.

While beginning to lament how much this luck of the draw would set Cole back over the course of the race, we were hit with an even bigger blow when a veterinarian came over to perform the mandatory checkup to ensure the dogs were healthy enough to compete.

The dogs were unloaded and tethered to the drop chains to begin getting on their harnesses and booties for the start. As the vet approached, I started to say, "Be careful. He's skittish," in regard to Wolf—who had developed quite a negative association with strangers, a result of the pain and trauma he endured during his recovery after being hit by a car—but the words left my lips too late. Wolf violently hurled himself under the truck to get away, and then whirled 180 degrees to keep a wary eye on this stranger with a dangling stethoscope.

I reeled Wolf out from underneath the truck, petting him, speaking to him soothingly, and making every effort to calm him down, but noticed that in the frantic dive between wheel and fender, he had caught his hip on a sharp edge. Where the loose skin of his thigh met his abdomen, he gave himself a huge laceration, pink and meaty, and not just through the skin, but deep into the muscle of his hind leg.

There was no way he could be outdoors in below-freezing temperatures with a wound like that, much less run on it. The race hadn't even started and Cole already had to drop a dog, and not just any dog, but an exceptionally hard driver and one of her main race leaders.

The vets were able to stitch Wolf up, which we were both thankful for, but starting the race with one less dog than everyone else weighed heavily on Cole's conscience, already overburdened with a litany of pre-race worries. Adding insult to the injury, we regularly bring an "alternate" in the truck in case something like this happened, but found ourselves lacking a spare race dog for the first time ever.

Metoo, still young, wasn't on this team, but usually accompanied us since she was fit enough to step in if we ever needed her, and because she hated us being out of her sight for more than a few minutes, much less days. But, she had wreaked havoc with the interior of the cab on more than one occasion when along for the ride, and we didn't let her run. Alas, for this trip, we opted to leave her home with the house sitter, and instead we took Shagoo and Buckwheat as copilots, neither of which could run due to medical conditions.

"I think there's someone named Murphy who has a law about this kind of thing," I said to Cole, trying my best to lighten the mood before a full funk could set in.

We soldiered on. Cole packed her sled while I continued with prepping the dogs, but as the race drew near, yet another problem presented itself. As the team that drew bib number one moved up, we realized the starting chute went right past our assigned parking spot. For dogs already excited to run, nothing pushes them into a full-blown state of frenzy like seeing others going first.

Every dog we had lost control. They howled hysterically, foamed rabidly at the mouth, and threw themselves to the end of their chain tethers with so much force that the truck swayed with each unison slam. Quigley, one of our dogs who is the canine equivalent of the muscle-bound lunkhead Lennie, from Steinbeck's *Of Mice and Men,* used his above-average strength to cannonball himself so hard that he broke a link in the end of the main drop chain, right where it connected to the truck.

With no equipment to crimp the chain back together, I resorted to holding the end of the chain to keep it taught and prevent the dogs tethered along the length from snaking out and interfering with the passing teams. This task was more than a tug of war; it was a test of attrition with the numbers being stacked seven to one. Not a winning proposition since I was that one, and had an hour-and-twenty-minute wait till Cole left the starting line. I dug my snow boot heels in, put my thighs into it, and leaned against the chain with all my strength, and hoped that Cole could get all the dogs geared up and hooked up to the sled before my stamina waned.

Somehow, we prevailed and Cole and her eleven-dog team made it out of the chute. Sopping with sweat and visible steam vapors rising off me, I was more than ready to sit in the truck for a few hours while motoring to the next checkpoint. I waited for the last team to go by, then slid into the driver's seat and turned the engine over. It rumbled to life, but also made a peculiar noise, shrill and unpleasant, like when someone accidentally steps on a cat's tail.

"That doesn't sound good," I said to Wolf, who nestled in my sleeping bag, which I had spread on the seat for him. He tilted his head inquisitively, then curled back up. Shagoo and Buckwheat were doing the same in the backseat.

The first few legs of the race brought the usual problems for Cole—a few bad passes with novice mushers driving inexperienced teams, a few dogs with sore muscles in her team, and overflow in the expected places—but nothing she hadn't experienced before, and nothing as horrendous as our prerace bad luck had been. Around the halfway point though, all that changed.

Roughly 160 miles into the race, I waited at the Wolverine Lodge checkpoint, a backcountry base camp for snowmachiners and mushers where the small friendly staff always seemed to have a warm bowl of stew or other hearty meal ready for weather-weary folks. The truck still emitted the sharp, eardrum-splitting sound—gradually becoming higher pitched—but otherwise showed no ill effects.

After seeing countless headlamps bobbing in through the darkness, to my delight one of them was finally Cole's. Astonishingly, she and the dogs looked like they had swum more than run to the checkpoint. The undersides of every dog were festooned with dangling gumball-sized ice clumps. It was clear they had been in water, deep water. Cole's appearance better confirmed how deep in the icy drink they went.

"There was a creek of open water about ten miles back. It was two feet deep, almost over the dogs' heads. In those temps they didn't want to get wet. I had to stand in the water and manually lift them across one-by-one," Cole explained.

She had a thin skin of ice up to her thighs and her boots were encased in solid blocks, including a frosty buildup on the soles that challenged her ability to stand squarely on the runners for those final miles. Her back and knees ached from the awkward riding stance she assumed, but worse still, standing in the bone-chilling cold of the creek for so long, the frigid water also seeped its way into her boots, soaking her socks and feet. She said she continuously wiggled her numb toes during the hour to the checkpoint, just to keep some feeling in them.

Once Cole fed and bedded the dogs down, she went in the lodge. After waiting several minutes for her boots to thaw, and chiseling at the laces during that time, she finally was able to break free from her frozen fetters. Popsicles fresh from the freezer looked more thawed than her blue-gray toes.

Having run the race before, she knew where a not-so-public dryer was located at the back of the lodge and loaded her clothes in to dry during her layover. After which, she quickly ate, then curled into the fetal position under a pool table to thaw out more and get what little sleep she could. I used the time to sneak a couple of French fries to my canine copilots—unperturbed by the still squealing sound of the running dog truck—then plodded over to monitor the race team's rest.

A few hours later, slightly past midnight, Cole suited up again and I followed her back outside to the biting cold. It was a still night and the scant bank of clouds in the sky quickly thinned, giving birth to an impossibly full moon. In its winter light, the snow glowed blue, making it easier for Cole to see as she bootied each dogs' paws. Minutes before she was scheduled to pull her hooks, the aurora began to radiate, its light green ribbons undulating high overhead.

Captivated, we stopped what we were doing, our eyes to the sky. Tendrils of steam rose from our nostrils with each exhale as we stood in silence and awe of the natural splendor likely few others besides us were witnessing. It was a moment that filled both of us with peace, after what had been a trying two days of racing.

Cole and the team departed without incident, but she decided to leave Penny—a small-statured yet steadfast lead dog—who had suffered a pulled muscle during the open-water-crossing fiasco. After mandatorily raking up the straw beds the dogs had slept in, I made my way back to the dog truck, now making a noise more like an electric drill than a running diesel engine. Penny settled in with the three other dogs already curled up in the cab. My plan entailed quickly making the 100-or-so-mile drive to the next checkpoint and grabbing a long overdue wink before Cole came in. Ten miles down the road, I realized I wouldn't be sleeping any time soon.

From under the hood came a confidence-crumbling loud snap, followed by an angry hiss. I didn't like the sound of either, and neither did the dogs riding with me. All four sprang out of their grogginess, looking alert and even more concerned than I did. Fearing being marooned in the middle of nowhere, I figured the best course of action was to try and press on, hopefully making it to a gas station in the next town, Glennallen, roughly thirty-three miles away. Within minutes, though, the engine began to overheat, billows of vapor blinding my view of the road, but I kept driving. Seconds later, the battery light came on signaling its death was now imminent. Still, I tried to push a little farther. But then, the steering and brakes went out. I had zero control and knew I was done for. The truck had completely conked out in the most cataclysmic way imaginable: a system-wide shutdown.

I got out and opened the hood. Once the scalding steam cleared I saw what looked like a pile of black spaghetti lying on the engine. It took me a few minutes to recognize it as the shredded remains of the serpentine belt—a long, snaking band of rubber that transports power to nearly all of the truck's vital components. It dawned on me that the sound I had been hearing for days was this belt about to give up the ghost. Worse still was the realization I didn't have a spare with me.

In the inky blackness of night I sat with a thousand-yard stare, rooting around in my mental attic trying to come up with an idea for what to do next. My options were bleak. I was on a road off the highway with no through traffic other than race-support crews, many of which were far ahead or behind me. It was too far, and in the still minus thirty temperatures, too cold to walk to town. I considered walking back to the checkpoint, but didn't want to leave the four dogs in the cab with no heat. I had a phone, but didn't know the numbers of anyone who could help. I felt like I needed a cigarette, an odd sensation since I don't smoke.

I decided the best course of action was to stay put and send for help with the next handler driving by. A friend of mine, John, was handling for another team that had been running a few hours behind Cole. I thought he might have a spare belt in his truck, or, could give me a lift to town. For the moment, though, I had to wait. The very vehicle that shattered my spirits was now my only shelter. Fearing it could also become an icy coffin, I put on all the clothes I brought and tucked into my sleeping bag with as many dogs as could fit in with me.

After shivering fitfully for close to an hour, a dog truck finally approached. At the first sound of its diesel engine growling in the stillness of the night, I ran into the road flapping my beaver-mittened arms wildly.

The driver of the truck slowed to a stop and rolled his window down suspiciously. He was a weathered-looking old man, with a long white beard and brow heavily wrinkled with creases, which I knew to be a contour map of his years mushing in the perpetually inhospitable climate that is winter this far north.

"'Ellow," he said, and I immediately recognized his accent as French-Canadian.

"Hello. Man, am I glad to see you. Do you speak English?"

"No," he said politely.

I felt myself slump a little bit, but was desperate to convey to this equally sleep-deprived handler what I needed. I decided, as all Americans do in these situations, to speak very slow and very loud.

"At the next checkpoint! The next checkpoint, yeah?" I shouted boorishly, pointing down the road. "I need you to find John! He's another handler, handler, like you. John! John the handler! Tell him I'm stuck here! Do you understand?"

"Yes," he said, nodding enthusiastically. "John. I find John."

"Yes, John," I shouted. "Give John this!" and I handed him a piece of paper I had scribbled my cell phone number on. With that, he pulled away into the night. I watched his glowing red taillights shrink in the distance, and I wondered if my message would get through. Forty-five minutes later I got an answer when my cell phone rang.

"Hello, this is John. I got a message to call this number," said the unfamiliar voice on the other end.

"Is this John Solem?"

"No, this is John Schandelmier."

My message got to John, just not the right one. Still, I explained my situation to this John, a handler for another musher in the race. He helpfully took the time to riffle around the auto shop at the lodge, but called back to say he had no luck in finding a serpentine belt. Committed to his own responsibilities, he had done all he could.

Still stranded, I continued to shudder uncontrollably in the dark and cold for two more hours. My sleeping bag was only rated to minus twenty and I felt the effect of it not having enough goose down to withstand the

Our dog truck caused lots of dilemmas over the years, but having a kennel full of dogs always helped us pull through the low times.

current mercury level. The inside of all the windows iced over from the condensation of breath, mine and the dogs'. The four of them curled tightly, their noses buried under their tails, but otherwise not concerned with the situation. I worried what Cole would do when she got to the next checkpoint and I wasn't there, but all negative thoughts ceased when I heard another dog truck coming, this time from the direction of the lodge.

In a stroke of luck it was someone who spoke English and that I knew, Sue Ellis, the wife of Mike Ellis, one of our close mushing friends from Fairbanks (and someone who holds views of animal ethics similar to our own). I explained the situation and she gave me a lift to the next checkpoint, so I could at least aid Cole and the team. I loaded the four dogs from my vehicle into my savior's truck and hopped in.

On the way through Glennallen, we passed one of the few automotive shops in town and despite it being only 4:00 A.M. I saw a wrecker pull in and the driver go inside and flip on the lights. We turned around and pulled in, but when I pushed the front door it was locked. After a few feverish knocks an elderly man in mechanics blue coveralls came to the door.

"We're not open yet," he said.

"Oh, sorry, it's just I'm in a bad way," I said and pleaded my sob story to him.

Taking pity, he let me come in while he looked up the belt size for my particular truck and sold me one off the wall. He said he normally would give me a lift back to the truck and help me put it on, but the only reason he had risen so early himself was a friend had called him at home after her car slipped off the icy road. He was on his way to go pull her out of the ditch and had already lost enough time helping me.

Sue and I got back on the road and about an hour later I arrived at the checkpoint with only ten minutes to spare before Cole and the team pulled in. Since this was the beginning of her third day racing, and an equal amount of time with almost no sleep, I didn't want her fatigue-muddled mind to focus on anything other than getting to the finish line, so I tried to keep the death of the dog truck a secret. Things went pretty well for a few hours, but toward the end of the break, someone who knew about my situation came by to lend support.

"Hey, I heard your truck broke down back near Wolverine. I can give you a lift over there after the race ends," he said. My eyes grew as big as snowballs, and Cole looked at me in confusion.

"The truck . . . isn't here?" she asked. "Is everything OK? What happened?"

With the cat out of the bag, I told this person I'd let him know and then explained the crummy circumstances to Cole. As I gave her the blow-by-blow, Brent Sass—who would later become the 2015 Yukon Quest champion, but at this moment in time was merely another musher parked next to her—heard the whole thing. He was also a friend from Fairbanks, whom Cole had raced many times. Brent, whose kennel motto has long been "attitude is everything," is the most jovial person I know. No amount of scornful weather, tough trail, or misfortune has ever gotten him down.

Basically, he's my polar opposite, which always makes him refreshing to be around, especially when times are tough.

"Ya know, my dad—who's here handling for me—is pretty good with mechanics. He keeps all my trucks running. I'm sure he'd be happy to give you a lift and help you get it running again," he said, completely unsolicited.

Like the help from the mechanic, the offer meant a lot, partially because it displayed the unwritten Code of the North, which is when someone is in need, you do whatever you can to help them. But Brent's gesture also moved me because he was currently closing in on the finish line and jockeying with a handful of close mushers for the win. He could have justifiably blown me off.

I found and introduced myself to Brent's dad, Mark Sass, and he was not only willing to help, but seemed genuinely excited at the prospect of lending a hand. He was essentially a taller, slightly older, and even more chipper version of his son. I left my four dogs in Sue's care and told Cole I likely wouldn't make the next checkpoint, but would try to be at the finish.

We got on the road and drove the 100 miles and several hours back to the truck, but as we lifted the hood in daylight, we—or really Mark—realized this wasn't going to be a quick fix.

"The belt didn't just go on its own. It looks like the bearings in one of your pulleys blew out and took the belt with it," he said, while hunched over the engine.

At this news, I felt my chest tighten, stomach churn, and ass leak a bit. This guy had already gone *way* out of his way to help me, but now, with a clear diagnosis pinpointing the pulley, I needed a ride thirty miles back to the auto-parts store in Glennallen *and* a lift back to the truck to put it in. I've wheedled for a lot in my time, but this was something I couldn't bring myself to ask this Good Samaritan, and lucky for me I didn't have to.

"Come on," Mark said. "If we hurry, we can get back to town, get the part, and get this truck running in time to see Brent and Colleen finish."

"Are you sure? You could just give me a ride to town and I could take a cab back to here," I said, trying to assuage my budding feelings of guilt.

"You're wasting time. Let's go," he said sternly.

I hopped in, and Mark made the drive back like he was trying to qualify for a Formula 1 team. We made it to Glennallen in record time and I went for a pulley. When I came out Mark was now under the hood of a broken-down Winnebago, helping the driver with a dead battery. I couldn't help but think there should be some kind of award for guys like Mark, since even in these parts, people like him—not just helpful, but truly selfless— are becoming fewer and farther between.

Once he had the Winnie up and running again, we broke the sound barrier back to my truck, got the old pulley off, the new pulley on, and the new serpentine belt in place. We were both so elated I thought we might hug, until I turned the ignition key.

Silence . . . still.

This time it was me who was able to troubleshoot my truck's tribulation. Having sat in minus thirty for the past ten or so hours, without running or being plugged in, the battery was now either dead or too cold to start. We tried jumping it off Mark's car, but it was a bust. My last nerve was becoming as threadbare as the belt I just replaced, and I could see from the scowl on Mark's mug that this situation was beginning to test even his infinite good spirit and stoic resolve to see this dilemma through to the end.

I remembered that on the way back from town the second time, about halfway between there and the truck, I had seen the dog truck belonging to Rick Swenson, who I heard—when last I saw Cole— had pulled out of the race at Wolverine. Exhausted from two days of racing, I speculated he probably pulled over to sleep for a few hours before driving home.

"He's got a battery charger," I said to Mark.

"Let's go," he said, and this time I knew better than to rebuff the offer.

Mark set a blistering pace there, and Rick, groggy at being awakened by us, let me use the charger despite having never met me. My bona fides of being "Colleen Robertia's husband" was good enough for him. Then, warp speed back to my truck where we attached the charger and despite my badgering that it *would* work, Mark still wouldn't abandon me until he was sure.

Fortunately for both of us, it didn't take longer than about twenty minutes to juice up the battery enough for the motor to turn over and the truck to run. At the first grumble of the engine, Mark bid me adieu.

"Sorry to rush off, but I don't want to miss Brent coming in and it'll be close if I'm going to make it as it is," he said.

"I understand completely and you've already done more than anyone would have. I sincerely can't thank you enough," I said, pumping his hand up and down in a vigorous shake, wishing there was more time for me to give him the lavish outpouring of gratitude I thought the man deserved.

"No problem," he said earnestly and without a hint of hubris.

He rolled his window up and sped off to cover the 116 miles to get to the finish line, and I left right behind him, but moving at a more reasonable speed. I wanted to rush too, but with everything that had already happened, the last thing I needed was to slide off the road and get stranded again. Plus, with the fear-adrenaline associated with fixing the truck in the past, a Novocain-high of total fatigue was starting to flood through my sleep-deprived body.

Over the hours it took to drive to the finish line, and then find and collect my four dogs from Sue, it dawned on me that I had not only slept a miniscule three hours in three days (those few winks coming before the dog-truck debacle), but I had managed to survive in that time on nothing but bad coffee, a greasy cheeseburger, and several handfuls of peanut butter cups. I never had time to change my clothes either, so after three days in the same socks and bunny boots, and stewing in the bodily juices associated with stress, I had developed a textbook case of trench foot and a level of odor hellacious enough to concern the Centers for Disease Control.

When I finally saw Cole at the finish, it was one of the few times I looked worse than she did at the end of a race. I felt my pulse beat again when I saw her place thirteenth, a respectable finish considering the caliber of mushers she competed with and the hardships the race doled out that year. I found Mark, ecstatic that he got to see Brent come in fourth.

I thanked Mark again, more profusely this time, but it still didn't feel like enough, so I asked Cole to nominate him during the race's finisher's banquet, when all mushers cast a vote for who should win the Sportsmanship Award. She agreed, and we were surprised to see some others had heard about Mark's good deeds, and nominated him too, but in the end, the race officials could only honor him verbally during the banquet, which they did, and the award went—as the rules dictate—to a musher in the race.

That Copper Basin 300 still stands out among all the mid-distance races Cole ran. It taught me that while you can't predict when an emergency will happen any more than you can prognosticate winning lottery numbers, you can be prepared for when things go mechanically wrong. I never drive anywhere without a spare serpentine belt in the truck, as well as a few other essential parts and automotive fluids.

The incident also taught me that a positive attitude can be half the battle. Sure, while we had a streak of horrendous luck during the race, every time a negative situation happened, something else positive occurred: people stopped and showed their kindness, helped in whatever way they could, and genuinely cared about more than their own priorities. Alaska is vast, but at its heart is a small, caring community.

The ordeal also made me realize that, in a way, handling mirrors life itself. Fundamentally, they're both about overcoming a series of obstacles, and the people who can best take all the trouncing without it completely crushing their soul are the ones who eventually prevail over their problems and triumphantly succeed at their goals.

Although, knowing a guy whose dad is mechanically inclined and willing to drive you several hundred miles in the dead of winter never hurts either.

Hammer to the Heart

I SIT STARING AT THE PHOTOGRAPH OF KAWLIJAH FOR A LONG TIME, as I always do on the anniversary of that sorrowful day. I run the tip of my forefinger over the image of him slowly, back and forth. The gesture represents the closest thing to petting him I can do now, years later.

From the start, Kawlijah (pronounced Kuh-LIE-juh) stood out as special. He had a unique deep-maroon pelage, a distinct and overtly loving personality, and in terms of performance he was raw power, like a hammer—and not a ball-peen or claw, but a sledgehammer—a fitting analogy in more ways than one, since Kawlijah's tragic end shattered our hearts to pieces.

He came into our lives homegrown from conception, from parents who stood out in their own right. His mother, Oaky, another husky in our kennel, made a name for herself at an early age by showing an incredible talent for leading. By a year old, she could gee and haw with surgical exactness, and always charged headlong into open creeks to fearlessly ford to the far side of the water. She also displayed a tireless stamina and could steadfastly maintain her speed over long distances. Even in the off-season when nearly all dogs get summer soft, Oaky's muscles rippled under her silky, cream-colored coat. Ever hopeful of going on a run, she would wail like a banshee anytime a four-wheeler—which she solely associated with training—cranked up for work or recreation.

Kawlijah, on the right, and his sister, Seeker, just a few hours old and nursing.
Kawlijah stood out as special from the very beginning.

Kawlijah's father, Crazy Horse, while well past his prime, was an equally amazing dog at his peak. He wouldn't take a step in lead, but as a swing dog (right behind the leaders) he excelled at gee-haw commands and could be counted on to steer the team where needed when the leaders were uncertain. He finished multiple Iditarods in his heyday, so his stamina and endurance were without question. He was an old-school husky, like what you'd envision in reading a Jack London tale, the kind you don't see much of anymore as mushers have bred in more hound-mixes, German short-haired pointers, and other sprint lines in recent years. Crazy Horse had feet like leather, was thick-bodied and even thicker-furred. He could weather even the worst Bering Sea storm without needing a running jacket or any other special protection.

To say Crazy Horse was beautiful would be like describing the *Mona Lisa* as just a painting of a woman. With the exception of his glacial blue eyes, white toe tips, and white star on his chest, he was almost entirely crimson-colored. We had other dogs in the kennel with varying shades of copper, rust, cinnamon, or carrot-orange coloring, but none with as rich, dark, and even-shaded a red coat as Crazy Horse had. His type of deep red was very rare and wholly captivating.

Red coloring in sled dogs isn't common due to the recessive nature of the genes that produce it. Many mushers find red dogs to be incredibly willful and hardheaded to train, so they aren't sought out as breeders very often. Still, from our personal experiences, while red dogs can be difficult to work with, once trained they are almost indestructible. They don't get hurt, they don't get tired, and they don't get bored or give up in long races. They just get stronger and stronger with each passing mile, all of which factored into our decision for using Crazy Horse as a sire.

Excitement grew within us as we waited impatiently for the weeks to pass. We endlessly wondered about the growing life in Oaky's womb, and of course, if any of her offspring would be red. After work, in the pastel world of Alaska's long-day sunsets, we would spend our evenings lying in the soft straw, petting Oaky. Just as phrenologists used to believe they could prognosticate intelligence through the feeling of bumps on the head, we ran our fingers through the downy fur of her growing belly hoping to predict how many pups we would soon be getting to know. Finally, after sixty-three days, on the evening of the summer solstice, as the scorching sun of the longest day dipped below the horizon, we got our answers.

Cole and I poked our heads in the whelping box when Oaky didn't come out to greet us for dinner. The sweet, earthy smell of birth hung heavy in the warm air, and we delighted in seeing her licking two tiny pups clean. One was a grayish female Oaky nosed gently to guide the wiggling, whimpering newborn to her first taste of mother's milk. We named her Seeker in the hopes she would one day find and follow trail like her mother. The other fuzz ball, a little round-bellied male already nursing, had to our great delight inherited his father's enchanting maroon hue from head to tail. Even his little leathery nose was liver-colored to the point of practically being purple. We named him Kawlijah after the "red man" from an old Hank Williams ballad.

We grew even more eager to get home from work. Each evening, as soon as they could walk, we took Kawlijah and his sister out to explore the world. We strolled through the garden where their olfactory senses were stimulated by all the earthy smells from the different vegetables and fragrant herbs, and Kawlijah loved playing hide-and-seek in the lush leaves of potato plants, weaving between the stalks like an agility dog running the poles, and pouncing out of the foliage to ambush his unsuspecting sister or mother.

By design, we explored other natural environments to encourage further foundational growth of minds and muscles. We visited the beach regularly to let them take in nosefuls of briny air, as well as to climb the soft, sloughing, sandy bluffs, some of which stood 125 feet high. At first, they awkwardly lumbered up the steep inclines and hesitantly eased their way back down, but within weeks they could scale even the sheerest sections with ease and finesse, and had developed enough balance and confidence to run downhill at astonishing speeds. We also brought the pups to the local swimming hole where they took to the gin-clear water like two tiny otters, staying close and cutting circles around us while the older dogs put in their usual laps across the pond.

We didn't know it at the time, but in those halcyon days our souls were already beginning to tie together. I wasn't yet a parent, but in Kawlijah I felt the same pride and joy that comes from knowing you have brought something wonderful into the world. He was beautiful, inside and out, and watching him grow, and learn, and transform away from the pudgy pup he started out as brought immense joy to our lives. Like a child, he felt like an extension of us. Whatever he would become, we would share in, becoming something new together. He embodied promise, for me, Cole, our team—for us all.

By a year old, Kawlijah really began to stand out. Males are often a little larger than females, but Kawlijah seemed to have a naturally muscular construction that made him look part pit bull or Rottweiler. With a thick neck, bulging shoulders, and beefy haunches, he was built like a brick outhouse, to use a mushing metaphor. Once plugged into the team and pulling, his build further burgeoned. His physique took on an even more athletic appearance, chiseled as a stone sculpture.

He took to sled dog life with exuberance. We typically run two teams at once when training, and utilize young dogs in the front of the chase team to capitalize on their natural predatory instincts to run after moving objects. Kawlijah excelled at leading this team, but he refused to run out front in the lead team. *Like father, like pup* we figured, and didn't let his red-dog obstinacy frustrate us. We've learned over the years that just because a dog isn't comfortable running in lead as a youngster doesn't mean they won't grow into the position at three, four, or five years old. It takes time for some dogs to develop the right mind-set.

Kawlijah would give 100 percent in any other place aside from lead: from the swing position behind the leaders, all the way back to the wheel position directly in front of the sled. He frequently ran in wheel, where he could use his brute strength to muscle the sled, navigating mazelike forests with tight corners where a weaker dog might allow it to clip a tree trunk or slide off an icy shelf. On uphill climbs, having him so close highlighted his abilities as an obvious asset. He drove hard, *really hard,* keeping his nose down, inches from the ground, to get more leverage while digging his clawed paws into the snow like crampons. This became his perpetual form on near-vertical terrain, a sight as impressive to behold as it was reassuring to have when forging trail toward a steep mountain's summit.

Kawlijah's yearling season fell simultaneous to Cole signing the team up for their first 1,000-mile race: the Yukon Quest. It would serve as a doozy of a test for a bunch of amateur animals. Running from White-horse, Yukon Territory, to Fairbanks, Alaska, the Quest is known as the "Toughest Sled Dog Race in the World" and rightly so. It traverses frozen rivers with car-sized blocks of jumble ice, climbs of nearly fictional pro-portions to wind-ravaged mountaintops with death-defying drops, and all during a time of winter when nights are seventeen hours long and temper-atures of forty below are considered average.

As the race drew near, one of our core race dogs suffered a minor but nagging sprain. Cole worried about how to fill the fourteen-dog roster for this ultramarathon. We evaluated our options, and while yearlings usually aren't the first choice for competing in a 1,000-mile race, we have known of a few outstanding dogs that have gone the distance. Kawlijah, as good at one year old as many of our seasoned adults, made the cut. Still, while Cole decided to start with him, she went into the race with the attitude of running conservatively to protect this youngster from overworking himself.

"I'll drop him at the first sign he isn't having fun," she promised, not that I would ever doubt she'd do anything but keep Kawlijah's—as well as all the dogs'—best interests in her heart and mind.

At the first checkpoint, Braeburn, a plowed field adjacent to a tiny truck stop roughly 100 miles into the race, Kawlijah made clear he was in his element. Cole pulled in, parked the team, performed her dog chores, then wandered into the restaurant to chow a hot meal and grab a few winks of sleep under a table. Kawlijah, though, wasn't just reluctant to relax; he downright refused to rest. Instead, Kawlijah hammered into his harness, throwing himself forward to force some momentum. He barked in volleys, for the *entire* first hour, and initially it entertained me. I enjoyed watching the great plumes of steam rising from Kawlijah's muzzle each time he carried on. Compared to my usual handler routine of sitting in silence, boredom, and cold, his tomfoolery served as a pleasant deviation . . . at least at first.

The older and more experienced dogs—after the usual meticulous pawing to get their straw beds just so, and worrying at their feet for a few minutes—curled up and slept, but Kawlijah acted more like a kid at its first slumber party. He stayed awake . . . the *entire* night. Disappointed he couldn't continue to run, he eventually acquiesced to the idea of stopping his antics and settled down, but still he refused to actually sleep. He tracked the constellations of checkpoint headlamps, shining and moving all around—on officials, media, spectators, and the foreheads of mushers tending to their teams. He sat and stared at the other dogs, listening to them lap their soaked kibble in the darkness. When that grew boring for him he tried to rouse a few dogs sleeping near him into play. Incensed that they ignored him, he simply resigned himself to gazing up at the neon-green luminescence of the aurora dancing in the celestial canopy overhead.

After six hours of rest, around 1:00 A.M. in the minus-thirty-degree morning, an apple-cheeked Cole began putting booties—protective Cordura footgear fastened with Velcro—on the dogs, which was a clear sign to

*Kawlijah, at a year old, handsome and
already as strong as many of the adult dogs.*

Kawlijah he would soon be running again. In anticipation, he became resurrected and exclaimed hallelujah as only he could. In a constant cacophony, Kawlijah boomed out every vocalization a dog can make, hysterically barking and bellowing, excitedly yipping and yowling.

He also lunged into his harness like a Clydesdale attempting to free a mired wagon. With teeth clenched around the gangline, he'd yank his head with mouthfuls of the braided rope, jerking the other still groggy dogs off-balance. When this didn't light a fire under Cole's behind, Kawlijah—who until that point had never chewed anything—began to not just pull, but actively chew through the main gangline. Knowing it would take him only seconds to buzz saw through, I shouted, but Cole couldn't hear me over the baying of all the dogs, now eager to get back on the trail. With strict race rules of no outside assistance, I began wildly gesticulating, my arms waving in all directions like an angry construction-crew foreman. Fortunately, Cole saw me pointing to Kawlijah, and stopped him before he set the whole team free.

At the second checkpoint, outside an elementary school in the Carmacks village made up of roughly 500 First Nations (Native) people and 200 miles into the race, Cole dropped Kawlijah from the team. She made the decision not because he was going mental, but because he had taken a bad step a few miles before, and showed signs of a slight pull to a shoulder muscle.

Although Cole decided Kawlijah shouldn't continue due to this injury, he wasn't fatigued and didn't understand why his race was over and he should be relegated to sitting on the sidelines with me while his buddies were still running and having fun. At the dog truck, still full of vim and vigor, he threw a tantrum of epic proportion. As the team pulled out of the checkpoint Kawlijah squealed sorrowfully and made every attempt to get back to his pack. He cannonballed so hard against the chain tethering him to the dog truck that the whole vehicle lurched, and emitted its own complaint in the form of a haunting metallic creak. He repeated this lunging attempt to rejoin his kennel mates at every subsequent checkpoint over the remaining 800 miles.

"I'm sorry, buddy. I know you don't get it, but it's for your own good.

It really is," I told him over and over, kneeling close and scratching him behind the ears to further comfort him. With his golden eyes, he'd stare into my soul trying to comprehend my meaning more than the words, and eventually would break the tension by lovingly licking my nose, perhaps his version of "let's agree to disagree."

The next year, Cole signed up for the Iditarod, which runs from Anchorage to Nome, and again Kawlijah earned a place among the sixteen dogs that started the race. Now as a two-year-old, the additional year of training better prepared him to be a part of one of these 1,000-mile ultra-marathons, and Kawlijah shined like a superstar.

Cole ran six to eight hours at a time, covering distances of 60 to 100 miles on each segment, and Kawlijah grew stronger with each passing mile. At one point, about two to three hours into a night run to Cripple—the official halfway point of the race—his oomph became blatantly obvious.

Cole's headlamp dimmed to nearly dead. The ultra-bright and ultra-light headlamps that are now the norm weren't yet available, and hers—more of a miner's style with a battery pack worn on the waist—had eight batteries to switch out. She parked the team, snacked the dogs, and then while standing at the front of the line, clicked her headlamp off and—despite being momentarily blind—raced to change out the batteries as quickly as she could.

It wasn't fast enough to Kawlijah.

In the pitch-black, Cole could hear him getting hysterical, and within seconds felt the bodies of the bulk of her team slam into her legs, nearly knocking her down. She feverishly finished the task at hand and when she clicked on her headlamp, she was surrounded by a tangled mess of dogs. Cole initially thought they had pulled the snowhooks loose, but as she frantically sorted out the mess, she realized the sled remained back where she left it, with only Kawlijah and Arrow, his ebony-colored partner, in wheel position.

Cole deduced that Kawlijah, like back on the Quest, had chewed on the gangline and this time successfully chomped cleanly through it. After several stressful minutes reuniting all the parts of her transportation, and hastily tying some half hitches and ring-bend knots, she was able to continue to the next checkpoint. There, rather than getting much-needed sleep, she spent her time braiding a better splice into her gangline and watching Kawlijah more closely from under a wrinkled brow.

In Nome, Kawlijah was among the fourteen dogs in Cole's string who finished the entire race and he stood out as the spunkiest by far, in our team or any other, despite having sojourned across Alaska. In the Nome dog lot—an icy, barren, and windswept area where teams are staked out next to plastic travel kennels while waiting for a flight out—Kawlijah refused to rest. Surrounded by a sea of huskies with heavy eyelids from so many days on the run, it was surreal to see him so awake, alert, and most worrisome of all, analyzing his situation for stimulation.

"It's like someone's been sneaking him espressos," I joked to Cole, but still weary from the trail and much more familiar with the pandemonium an agitator like Kawlijah could create when bored, she made her own somber observation (a prediction really).

"That dog is going to cause trouble before we leave here," she said.

Kawlijah had, at an early age, figured out that if he backed up to the end of his tether, and then shimmied his head back and forth, he could loosen even the tightest collar and slip out. He did this dozens of times at home. Because of this, in the yard Kawlijah would wear a cinch-style collar unless he was running in the team, but we had forgotten to pack this neck restraint for Nome. So, several times a day Kawlijah worked his way to freedom, then farcically cavorted around the dog lot working all the other dogs into full hysteria, until we, or some annoyed volunteer, could chase him down and tackle him. He made a lasting impression on many passers-by who happened to be standing there when he broke loose, and the Iditarod staff working the dog lot quickly came to know him by name.

We ended up putting two collars on him, so that one collar would catch and bind on the other when he tried his usual reversal trick. This slowed his escape antics, but since he couldn't get it off, he would wail, run in endless circles, and jump on and off his crate in the dog lot to make sure everyone knew how displeased he felt about his dilemma. Among the stilled silence of the other sleeping dogs, Kawlijah stood out like a fiery-red shooting star streaking through the sky on a quiet night. Numerous mushers inquired about buying or breeding to what they could tell was an out-standing and clearly tireless dog. There were several long faces when we informed these folks that Kawlijah was already neutered and not for sale.

Based on his performance as a two-year-old, Cole and I beamed at the prospects of what Kawlijah would be like as an adult, since distance sled dogs typically don't hit their peak until three to seven years old. The whole flight home from Nome after the race, we talked about all the possibilities and contributions Kawlijah would make in the coming years. Sadly, it was not to be, and that Iditarod ended up being our sweet boy's last run.

Chalk it up to God, fate, coincidence . . . whatever you believe in, some force of nature acted just days after we got home, I believe, to per-sonally remind me of what is truly important in life. I have for years val-ued nothing as more important in my life than my wife, daughter, and our dogs. We are "one of those types" who view our dogs as part of the family, our canine kids. I believe *nothing* should come before the things you love, and our protective nature for our dogs has meant that Cole and I rarely leave the state together for business, family reunions, or vacations. And I definitely would not choose work over my dogs' well-being.

However, at that time, a new, micromanaging, pustule-of-a-boss at my work had been causing massive problems for me due to a conflict of personalities. In the days after Iditarod, things reached a boiling point, and on this fateful morning, in a desperate attempt to keep my job, I needed to hurry in early to speak with a human resources agent on East Coast time.

Adding to the situation, after returning home from Nome, our house remained a cluttered ruin from the fever of last minute packing and hosting company that flew north for the race start, but we immediately went back to work before anything could be cleaned and organized. We couldn't find Kawlijah's cinch collar. Worse still, his usual location in the dog yard had flooded with melting snow from spring breakup, and after being moved to a new spot while his usual abode dried out, he began slip-ping his collar regularly. I worried he would do his Houdini act while we were gone for an eight-hour workday, and end up getting out to the road and hit by a car.

In a rush to get to work, I put Kawlijah in our chain-link puppy pen until we could get home and find the correct collar. It was a roughly ten-foot-by-ten-foot square with the fencing standing about six feet high. Raised in this pen during his puppyhood, and later spending time in there to play with other dogs, he had never had a problem. But now, alone and unhappy to be away from us and his pack mates, he must have felt stifled. He had, after all, just gone from running almost all day long in the Iditarod to being asked to sit around while we went back to work, and his history proved he never did well transitioning to newfound downtime.

Being his usual energetic self, he must have been jumping around the pen, or more likely, attempting to leap out. With the additional height of the snow that had accumulated in the pen through winter, he apparently jumped high enough to catch his collar on the top of a rung of chain-link. The little metal triangular teeth would normally not even be glanced at twice as something dangerous, but on this ill-fated day one bit like a vicious animal. It suspended Kawlijah off the ground. He must have spun in an attempt to get down, but it was clear the collar twisted. It tightened on his windpipe, choking him. It cut off all breath. All life. His life.

Kawlijah hanged himself.

It was a helpless, helpless feeling to come to that realization. By the time we got home his body was cold and stiff. His tongue, that just that morning licked our faces in a warm, wet good-bye, was now dry, dangling, swollen, and purple. Beneath him lay a pile of bloody stool from where he fought so violently and so valiantly just to stay alive.

The happiest, most beautiful dog in the kennel was dead.

Our superstar was dead.

A beloved member of our family was dead, and it had not been a good death.

Rather than being there to save a dog that in all likelihood was trying to get out to find and be with us, I was at work defending myself from false accusations at a job I hadn't cared about in years. Riddled with guilt, I quit the next day, but it offered little closure. I still felt as if the weight of the world had fallen on me.

A dark, cavernously deep despair consumed Cole and me both. The pain burned like radiation, invisible to people coming to pay their condolences. They couldn't see it, but it was there. The hurt. It made me sick to my stomach, charred my heart, seared me soul deep.

Worse still than bearing the burden of anguish no one other than Cole seemed to comprehend the magnitude of were the conversations whenever I let a little of the sorrow out and confessed to someone my feelings about what had happened. Most didn't understand. Our society reserves grieving for other humans: fathers, mothers, husbands, wives, so on and so forth. We are expected to feel sad when we lose a pet, but not truly mourn the loss of life, particularly not men.

Men are allowed to follow sports with mindless enthusiasm and sulk for extended periods when one of the arbitrary games doesn't end with the odds in their team's favor, but we're not supposed to be emotionally hamstrung for weeks after finding the swaying corpse of a four-legged friend.

"You just need to get over it," would be the typical response, and as insensitive as the words were to hear, they were far less painful than those who did try harder. In a macabre sense of sharing, it surprised me to find out upon hearing what had happened to Kawlijah how many people's first reaction was to tell me about a canine tragedy they had experienced.

"I had a dog hang himself too. He jumped over a fence while tied up and the chain wasn't long enough for him to reach the ground on the other side," someone told me, almost matter-of-factly.

Were these stories for me or them? How could they say those words with so little emotion? We both had in common the death of a dog, but was their apparent lack of feeling because of how much time had passed or because their pet didn't mean as much to them? I couldn't be sure.

Then there were the well-intentioned folks who tried to come at my anguish more analytically, citing the five stages of grief: denial, anger, bargaining, depression, and ultimately acceptance. I was told to expect and accept these emotions, and I initially believed that like a dog race, if I just hung on and endured to the end, I would overcome these emotional obstacles over time and eventually cross a finish line to feeling whole again. But life isn't a psychology textbook; torment doesn't flow in a predictable path or abate in prescribed increments. I had other dogs die before and since

Kawlijah—some peacefully from natural causes and some from painful diseases long before their time should have been up—but none have left me as addled, as afflicted, as aggrieved as his passing.

It was a cruel, sick irony that this dog was in the pen that day because of slipping his collar countless times, but couldn't do it one last time when it really counted. Kawlijah was dead, and he died alone, likely scared, most definitely suffering for the last few minutes he remained conscious. We weren't there to comfort him. To help him. To save him.

Huskies are a breed not known for being as friendly as, say Labradors, but Kawlijah's personality publicized loudly and proudly that he remained a puppy at heart. Despite his brawny build and raw power in the team, outside of wearing the harness Kawlijah was so customarily jovial and so ridiculously gregarious that just about every family member, kennel friend, and fan who came for a visit or saw him at a race came to know and recognize him personally. Everywhere he went he elicited smiles and laughs simply by being himself.

It's been years since that horrible day, and while I would do anything to get this greeting from him again, one of the regrets that haunts me most—other than putting him in that pen that morning—was the night before he died, as I came in from doing chores, he tried to give me his version of "hugs and kisses." With an astonishingly gentle touch, he would stand on his hind legs, put his front paws on my shoulders, and softly lick my face.

This gesture was one of his favorites—mine too—but tired from a long day defending myself at work and stressed about going in the next morning to more office politics, I waved him off. True to his good-natured spirit, he didn't hold it against me. He merely wandered to a dog bed on the other side of the room, curled up, and watched me brood. There, he wagged his tail in soft little thumps, still excited at sharing the same space with Cole and me for the evening. That was enough for him, to be near us. I wish I had done more that night than ignore him and worry about problems that less than twenty-four hours later would be seen for how completely insignificant they really were.

I'm filled with sorrow that we never got to see him develop and grow, and reach his peak and full potential, but mostly I'm sorry I wasn't there for him. I would quit any job, drain my bank account, sell my soul—basically do anything I could to have that fateful day over again, to not put him in that pen, to have him back. He'll never know, never *could* know, the hole he left in our lives and in my heart. I held him in my hand, a small ball of maroon fur when he was one hour old, and it was way too soon when I cradled his lifeless corpse in my arms on his final day.

After we found him dead, I carried him in the house and laid him on a dog bed in front of the woodstove. For hours, Cole and I hugged his body, turned stiff as wood with rigor mortis. We ran our fingers through his beautiful red coat giving him pets that could no longer be felt, and whispering confessions of guilt and remorse into ears that could no longer hear.

We never forgot the texture of that tragedy, never healed from the loss of Kawlijah's untimely death. We just learned to live with the pain. As the English poet and novelist D. H. Lawrence one said, "We've got to live, no matter how many skies have fallen." And we did.

We continued our lives, because we had to, for the other forty dogs. It was catharsis, really. After learning the lesson of how quickly any of them could be taken from us forever, we became even better caretakers to them, savoring every minute with each one.

While Kawlijah's time on Earth was brief, I am immensely thankful to have known him. He was deeply loved and is sorely missed, as a superstar athlete, a loving pet, and one of my best friends, human or canine alike.

To this day, every time the whole yard howls at dusk, and I let what has to me become the most natural sound in the world wash over me like the wind, I still find myself longing to hear his voice among them. But, it only exists in my memories and in my heart. And the only place I can see his endearing face is in photographs, of which there are far too few. Far too few.

The Race Isn't the Only Obstacle

THE SNOWFALL HAD LONG SWITCHED FROM FULL WHITEOUT conditions to an are-we-going-to-be-buried-alive storm. I could no longer see any sign of a paved path, the glow of taillights just a few yards in front of us, or the guardrails along the side of the highway. I rolled my window down and stuck out my head, squinting through the white material that stingingly pelted my face. I couldn't even distinguish the front end of the truck hood. Cole scanned out the passenger window, hoping to help guide me from that side, but in that moment the four-lane highway's width appeared as an infinite expanse.

Suddenly head-on headlights materialized right in front of us, but luckily the vehicle was traveling at a snail's pace. I realized I had unknowingly migrated to the farthest of the oncoming lanes, and so slowly swerved my way back to what I perceived as the correct side of the road.

With this close call, the fear that had been building for hours was now palpable from everyone riding in the cab of my truck. All conversation stopped or turned laconic. It basically boiled down to Cole's uncle—whose normally California-tan face was now color-flushed and whiter than the falling snow—saying as soothingly as possible, "You're doing fine, Joseph," every two minutes on the dot. It was a mantra he seemed to be using to reassure himself as much as lend moral support to me, and when he wasn't verbally ticcing, the only sounds heard were the monotonous beat of the windshield wipers and the hum of the heater blowing stale air.

The mood was sour enough from everyone riding thigh-to-thigh and shoulder-to-shoulder, since we had crammed five adults into a space built for three at most. The ambience worsened when it became clear—due to the road conditions—we couldn't safely stop for a bathroom break despite everyone consuming twenty-ounce lattes at the start of the road trip, and that our only sustenance during the long drive—a stale can of pickle-flavored Pringles—had long been exhausted.

Still, I sustained a focus sharp enough to split atoms, and tried to hide my own anxiety, but my passengers saw through the performance of bravado when at one point I swallowed and my throat made an audible click. I scanned in the rearview mirror to survey the scene in the cab and frozen on everyone's faces were grimaces the likes of which I hadn't seen since fifth grade when the class was subjected to the "Miracles of Childbirth" video for the first time.

I knew it was time to come clean, so I did with one honest statement, "Everyone . . . I'm not sure we're going make it."

Tales are legion of all the things that can go wrong during the Iditarod and other sled-dog races, but few and far between are the stories of all the misadventures that happen on the run-up to, and in those few days after the race, when mushers are still miles from the comfort of home and the security of a regular kennel routine.

For Cole's first Iditarod, as only days remained till the start, she suffered the usual rookie symptoms: a belly full of butterflies, hard anxiety lines across her forehead, and her thoughts were a revolving door for what-if worries about all the possible calamities that could occur over the next two weeks of racing. And not without good reason. More people have stood on the summit of Mount Everest than successfully driven a dog team from Anchorage to Nome.

We were trying to head off any and all problems before they could present themselves, and one of the dilemmas many mushers face is that the race requires rookies to be in Anchorage for nearly the full week before the big day. It's mostly to meet about the trail, review dog care techniques, and learn etiquette for interacting with the press, but competitors also face a fair share of autograph-signing events and posing for pictures with fans from around the world.

For mushers from Outside of Alaska, this week in the city tends to be a disadvantage. Many folks fly their dogs into Anchorage crammed in crate-like kennels or by driving with them cramped in a dog box on their truck or trailer, and sadly, these abodes are where these canine athletes end up staying for those final days before beginning their ultramarathon.

This seemed like a poor decision to us. You'd never see athletes attempting similar endeavors, such as Tour de France cyclists or Ironman contenders, spending the week before their competitions curled in the fetal position in something the size of a suitcase.

Wanting to avoid these inferior accommodations for Cole's race team, we decided I would stay at home in Kasilof with the dogs for the week so they could keep to their normal routine as long as possible, sleep in their own roomier doghouses, and continue to do short training runs to keep them limber. This meant that on Friday, the day before the start of the race and Cole's only day "off" from Iditarod-related duties that week, I would drive the roughly 175 miles north and get her. We would then drive home together, that afternoon, load the dogs up and then drive back that night to minimize their time in the dog boxes of the dog truck. This much commuting would normally equate to around ten hours of total travel time, at least when all the stars aligned.

Adding to the logistical insanity, since this was Cole's inaugural running of the Last Great Race, several members of her family flew up to see her off. When I got to Anchorage that Friday, Cole's Uncle Jeff and her brother and sister, Ross and Russet, decided to ride back down with us to our kennel to see our home and the whole dog operation. We even promised her uncle, visiting from Los Angeles, a quick sled ride with some of the dogs not slated for the Iditarod, which is how we all came to be together in the two-wheel drive sardine can I had driven up.

As a kid growing up, I heard the old cliché that "Eskimos" had more than 100 words for snow, something I never really understood until I came to Alaska. After living in the far north for a few years, I quickly began to appreciate their specificity once I realized there truly are a lot of different types of snow. There's heavy, wet snow that falls in feather-sized flakes, and light, dry snow that delicately dances down to earth. There's sticky snow for building snowmen, and dry snow that squeaks and crunches under every bootfall. Accumulations can be powdery or packed. Corn snow forms in little balls, while sugar snow has the appearance of loose sand. And sometimes snow that is silky smooth can, with a rise of just a few degrees, transform into a sloppy and slushy mess within minutes.

The list goes on and on, and while I thought I had experienced every type of snow in my time as a dog musher, what we were attempting to drive through was an entirely new environmental occurrence. Perhaps Natives need to add the term "buttload" to their lexicon.

The storm dropped *so* much *so* quickly, at least a foot of snow an hour. I felt like we were caught in the winter equivalent of a flash flood, and before we were even a quarter of the way to the kennel, the deep accumulations slowed our speed to fifteen miles per hour. Several cars in front of us turned tail and headed back to the big city, but we didn't have that option.

We had to make it.

No matter what.

We pressed on, fearing if the squall was this severe at our current lower elevation, what the heck would it be like when the highway moved to its highest point through a mountain area known to Alaskans as "The Pass." We quickly found out.

As the roadway incline increased and proceeded farther up, the visibility somehow worsened. The side of the road grew littered with cars and trucks that had gotten sucked into the deeper powder just off the paved surface. They were the only color. Everything else was white, and I mean whiter than wearing fanny packs or watching *Friends*. It was live-audience-for-*A-Prairie-Home-Companion* white.

I briefly entertained the idea of pulling over to wait the storm out or loiter a bit until a snowplow came by, but in a two-wheel-drive vehicle, I knew if we stopped for any reason we'd need a tow to get going again, and based on the number of socked-in vehicles we had already passed, I knew the wait for a wrecker would be a long time coming. So we pressed on.

Fortunately, after we crested the pass and began our descent down the far side of the mountain, we left the worst of the weather behind. Before long the snow tapered, the road and landscape along the way became visible again, and the sky shifted from opaque white to its usual slate-gray. We all became giddy once we realized we were going to survive, and downright gleeful once we finally hit a section safe enough to pull over to pee. We eventually made it to the kennel, but the trek took more than five hours.

AT THE KENNEL AND NOW RUNNING LATE, WE SPRANG INTO ACTION. Cole, with help from her siblings, began packing the dog truck with all the gear she would leave the starting chute with, while I honored my promise to give her uncle a quick sled ride. I swiftly harnessed and hooked up several young dogs and shot out of the yard with Jeff in the sled bag.

My plan was a simple one: just run our puppy loop, which is only three miles long and typically takes no more than fifteen minutes. I was pleased to realize the edge of the harrowing storm we commuted through the heart of stretched to our home turf. It spread a thin sheet of new snow that made for perfect tour conditions.

Whizzing down the trail behind a team of hyped-up huskies, past spruce boughs slumping under their heavy accumulations of fresh snowflakes, flanked by leafless birches with an inch or two of white stuff clinging to every bend of their branches all the way down to their thin tiny tips, and with the brisk, fresh air flowing in our faces—all the stress of the morning washed away, from myself, and Uncle Jeff. The antithesis of the typical urban dwelling, Jeff openly shared his awe of all that we have in abundance from living life in Alaska: the enormous openness, the isolation that quickly comes with it, and the intoxicating tranquillity of traveling through all this remarkable country by dog team.

Simply savoring the moment was more than enough for him, but I wanted to put a real exclamation point on his Alaskan experience, so for the final half mile, I decided to switch positions and let Jeff mush the remainder.

Swapping places wasn't anything new, really. Short of infants, invalids, and imbeciles, we usually let people drive the homestretch because the dogs, having had some gas siphoned off over the course of the tour, are less unruly. They know where they're headed and that the fun is almost over. Also, it's basically a straight line back to the kennel, so driving doesn't really require any sled-handling skills or even balance. It only requires that the person hang on.

I stopped, set the snowhooks, exchanged positions with Jeff, and explained, in order, the short list of tasks needed to get us going again. I had even taken Jeff's camera—a new, top-of-the-line Nikon—so I could get a dynamic in-the-bag point-of-view photograph of him driving his first dog team. Like everyone, he was hesitant to take over, but too excited to say no.

"So all I have to do is pull up this hook and say, 'Hike,' right?" he asked.

"That's it, and just say it like you mean it so the leaders up front can hear ya," I said reassuringly. "That's all you gotta do, that and hold on."

To be fair, that's exactly what Jeff did, yet the plan—much like the sled—fell apart in an impressively memorable manner.

Jeff, while not huge, is a much more well-upholstered man than myself, by at least 100 pounds or so. Added to this, the sled we took out—a garage-sale special—was a rickety thing that creaked louder than the hinges on my outhouse door.

As Jeff pulled up the snowhooks and shouted "Hike," from behind my head I heard a calamitous cracking sound. Instantaneously, the dogs, and the sled with me still in it, accelerated from zero to twenty miles per hour. Looking over my shoulder I could see Jeff getting smaller in the distance, still standing right where we had been, the handle-bow of the sled still clenched in his mittens, and with a wide-eyed look on his face much like a man makes during his first proctology examination.

Normally, I would have rolled out of the sled, hanging on to the support stanchions, while trying to stomp the brakes. However, when the handle-bow broke off in Jeff's hands, the sled lurched to the side, and dumped me out, but I managed to hold on with one hand. With the other I hoisted Jeff's Nikon as high as I could to protect it from the limbs and tree trunks along the trail's edge that battered me at high speed while I dragged. With no one to steer the sled, slow it, or stop it, I went careening down the trail looking more like an overturned bobsled.

I knew my body couldn't keep absorbing the full force of the impact against trees, but I was incapable of climbing back into the sled while holding the camera, and I refused to throw Jeff's expensive new Nikon into the snow. I had to let go—one of only three times I have ever relinquished my grip on a sled and the only time outside my first year when I still lacked face-planting panache.

I stood up, ran back fifty yards or so toward Jeff, tossed him his camera, and then took off in a full sprint after the dogs—never an easy feat in bunny boots and multiple layers of bulky, insulated clothing. I knew the dogs were within a half mile of the kennel, but still, letting go of the sled can lead to dangerous tangles where a dog could be hurt or possibly killed if a line looped around their neck or torso.

Back at the house, Cole stood in the yard cutting salmon on our band saw. The humming motor masked the approaching sound of the team, and her first indication of any problem came when she felt a nudge at the back of her legs. She turned and saw my whole team—panting, slightly tangled, and all eagerly waiting for chunks of the frozen pink meat she had just been slicing.

"Stop what you're doing!" she shouted to her brother and sister, who were scooping poop. "The dogs just came back without Joseph or Jeff!"

They didn't know what this meant exactly, but by the look on Cole's face and the panic in her voice they could tell something was seriously wrong. They threw down their shovels and rakes and, after Cole briefly barked what to do, they sorted out my snarled team and unhooked dogs from their lines. Cole then dashed out of the yard hoping to get a glimpse of us to determine what happened. Within a few dozen yards she met up with me. Completely out of breath, I managed to choke out between deep ventilations, "Everyone's . . . " *huff, huff,* "totally . . . " *huff, huff,* "fine."

Jeff staggered in a few minutes later, his face red, brow beaded with sweat, sucking wind as if breathing through a straw, his camera in one hand and the handle-bow in the other. When everyone's respiration returned to normal, we described what happened from our own perspectives and briefly had a good laugh about it. With no more time to spare, we loaded up the last of Cole's stuff and the dogs, and we got underway for the return trip to Anchorage, this time in the four-wheel-drive dog truck with studded snow tires.

THE STORM THAT PLAGUED US ON THE WAY DOWN COMPLETELY abated in the time we were at home, and the snowplows had removed the worst of the deep powder from the roadway. We made it back in the usual three hours and rolled in just as the sun—finally visible for the first time that day—set behind the snowcapped Chugach Mountains that skirt the city's edge.

Weary from the adrenaline peaks and valleys of the day, we were all eager to get to our rooms in one of the higher-end hotels in the heart of the city. Jeff had sprung for them so we could all be close together and near to the starting line in order to get a little more sleep before the big day. We were looking forward to turning in early so we'd be well rested for the next morning's ceremonial start through downtown. Cole and I retired to our suite, saying our goodnights in the elevator, while Jeff rode up another few floors to the room he had, earlier that day, checked into and left his luggage in. When he stepped off the elevator, he saw two teens in baggy clothes feverishly attempting to gain access to the same suite he was headed for.

"Is that your room?" he asked them.

"Yeah," one grunted back.

"Oh, I must have gotten off on the wrong floor," Jeff said, thinking his weariness from the day's event must have snuck up on him.

He turned to leave, but double-checked his key card, and realized he was, in fact, on the correct floor. Thinking *they* must have had the wrong floor, he went back and found them still at the door, repetitively and unsuccessfully trying their electronic key card.

"Are you guys sure this is your room?" he queried again.

"Yeah, our stuff's in there," one said.

"That's weird. I'm pretty sure this is my room. Maybe the hotel double-booked it. What's your name? I'll go down to the front desk and sort it out."

"Jeff Morrow," said one of the kids.

"Jeff . . . Morrow?" Jeff asked in disbelief. "That's my name."

Something about this *did not* sit right.

Down at the front desk, Jeff explained the situation and the employee understood all too well what had happened. He called the police and then explained the grift to Jeff. Apparently, some unscrupulous folks will rent a room, then keep one of the electronic key cards to periodically retry it in the same room, knowing that the hotel has some form of revolving system such that, after enough time has passed, the old key cards will work again.

The concierge—a well-dressed, dandyish man with an oversized smile that silently screamed "please don't sue us"—dispatched hotel security forthwith to apprehend the two hoodlums until police arrived to take them to jail. As they were hauled off, one of them brazenly bragged how he had just been released from the slammer less than twenty-four hours earlier, after several months of detainment.

And here I thought our luck had been rotten that day.

The hotel staff opened Jeff's room and we all went in to assess what had been taken or damaged. We were rendered speechless when we saw how at home they had made themselves, a queer act considering they had to know someone else was in that room too, and would be coming back at some point.

These scofflaws had made numerous calls on Jeff's cell phone and there was an assorted pile of swag obviously stolen from vehicles during the day. This consisted of some camera equipment, some high-end bicycle parts, a (pried-open) briefcase filled with legal documents, and a duffel bag stuffed with hundreds of pink and blue artificial sweetener packets, like those found on a table in a diner. Countless empty energy drink cans littered the room; apparently sugary liquid stimulants had been their main sustenance. On one wall, one of the culprits had assembled a photo collage with no less than thirty prints of himself and a lady friend of his, in various poses of amorous affection.

The truly wacky part, though, was that they had taken off much of their own clothing to wear Jeff's, not only far from the correct size for them or even remotely fitting their thug stylings, but most of it inexplicably included his dirty clothes that they had put on from an obvious discard pile. Oddly, when apprehended, one of them had even donned a pair of his sweaty, unwashed dress socks.

As weird as the evening ended up, the hotel, being very apologetic and wanting to keep this sort of incident as hush-hush as possible, compensated Jeff for his stay. We didn't turn in early like we had hoped, but we all were thankful that the day's events had at least, for a few hours, gotten Cole's mind off worrying about her first Iditarod.

COLE WENT ON TO HAVE A GREAT RACE. SHE FINISHED A LITTLE MORE than ten days later, in thirty-sixth place, with fourteen of the sixteen dogs she had started with. Not too shabby for a rookie run. Two years later she followed up with an even more impressive twenty-first-place finish, and while her inaugural run was marked by bizarreness before the race, her second running was followed by some equally surreal situations.

That year, I flew into Nome, the terminus of the Iditarod, a few days early to try to find accommodations in the coastal community. If it sounds ridiculous to wait until the last minute, I agree. We normally don't, but both times we had counted on Iditarod organizers to do as they promised and find Cole a homestay and both times they hadn't come through.

Nome's a tiny town, only about 12.5 square miles of land. A handful of businesses are sprinkled down the main thoroughfares, of which it seems every third one is a bar or liquor store. The few hotels accommodate as many visitors as they can, but there's simply not enough space for every musher and their families and friends, and throngs of officials, sponsors, media, fans, etc. The rooms book up as early as a year out, and even then, reserving a room doesn't mean the proprietors won't give it to someone who bids higher when the race finally comes to town.

The race attempts to arrange homestays for mushers, but like the hotels, not everyone wants a musher in their abode for a few days. I'd guess a lot of people have been rubbed the wrong way over the years—by ungrateful and at times egotistical organizers, as well as weary mushers tracking in dog poop, among myriad other problems. A few Nomeites are hospitable enough to open their homes for a few days, but these places—whether by their own choice or the Iditarod's own preferential treatment for its celebrities—always seem to go to the big name mushers.

The first year Cole ran, we got lucky. She finished far enough back that some of the front runners had already flown home, so we were able to rent for the week a simple, sparsely furnished apartment at the rate of $100 a day. This may seem excessive, but is actually pretty fair as postrace price-gouging goes. Our only real complaint was that the roof leaked steadily from all the melting snow, soaking our bed in ice-cold water the first night, but after we pushed the mattress to the far side of the room the remainder of our stay was adequate.

On her second running we were not so fortunate. Upon arriving, I spent a day haggling with Iditarod staff over finding us a homestay. Their only offering was miles outside of town, on the floor, and it would be shared with several other mushers. While floor space is better than camping on the ice, Cole had been roughing it for a week and a half and I strongly believed she deserved better than that. I also knew she would want to be closer to the dogs to check on them several times a day.

After too many hours of chasing my own tail, I found accommodations in the only place with any vacancy, above the raunchiest and most raucous bar in town. The place was a real *Shitz*-Carlton, and our room—with its aromatic blend of mildew and stale cigarette smoke, and looking like it hadn't been thoroughly cleaned since perms and acid-wash jeans were in style—had all the ambience of a jail cell. It was literally not much larger than a bathroom stall, yet oddly enough didn't have a toilet of its own. There were two communal bathrooms on the floor, but one had already backed up and so, as a crudely handwritten note informed us, was "shut down until further notice." The other lavatory shared a common, paper-thin wall with our room, which allowed us to hear a disgusting symphony of stool plopping and flushing seemingly twenty-four hours a day.

Luckily Cole arrived the night after the wet T-shirt contest in the bar below our room, which—between the blaring music of the live band,

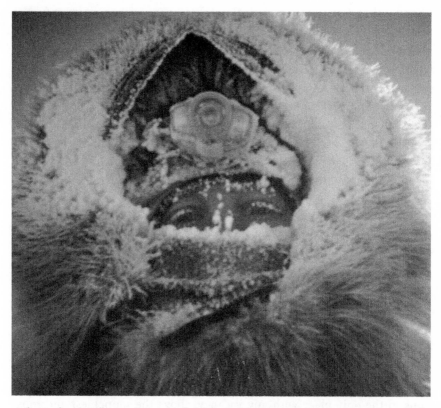

A frosty-faced Colleen nearing the finish line of the Iditarod. We found out on multiple occasions that completing an event didn't mean the adversities were over—we've experienced practically everything that could go wrong before and after races.

the horny hollering and catcalls of men, and the occasional giddy shriek of a woman having who knows what done to her—I slept very little.

The next morning I awoke and went to the sole bathroom to find there was no toilet paper anywhere in sight. I started down the hall, but on my way to the front desk to scare up some toiletries, I bumped into a clean-cut Native man stepping out of one of the rooms. Since many residents of Nome are Native, but most of the people I had encountered in hotels were non-Native tourists, I assumed this man worked for housekeeping.

Wrong!

"Hey, any chance of getting some more toilet paper in the bathroom?" I asked.

He stared dumbfounded for a few seconds, but then an indignant look grew upon his face. Realizing my mistake—and I can only assume thinking I was a huge racist (which I'm not, I swear I'm not)—he squinted at me and hissed, "I don't fucking work here," and then curtly shouldered his way past me.

I thought of chasing him down to tell him I held no ill will toward any ethnicity but was suffering from sleep deprivation (and possibly posttraumatic stress) due to the horror of hearing sphincters of varying shutter speeds all night long. Embarrassed enough, I decided instead to make my way to the first floor.

There, I found the room-service woman pushing her cleaning cart. She was also Native, in her late forties and a little haggard looking, but unlike the man upstairs who was reasonably well-dressed, her work attire consisted of a pair of dirty sneakers, jeans with holes in the knees, and a T-shirt that read, "Happiness is a tight pussy."

How had I ever made the mistake?

Wanting to ease into my request after crashing and burning with the case of mistaken identity upstairs, in my most polite voice I asked, "Excuse me, ma'am, not sure if you're aware, but there's no toilet paper on the second floor."

"Yeah, yeah," she said gruffly, while not making eye contact with me and rubbing her temples. "I'm a little hungover from the wet T-shirt contest last night, so I'm moving slow. I'll get there when I get there."

On that note she ended our conversation. With nothing left to say to anyone else, and feeling like I had significantly set back cultural relations between Caucasians and Alaska Natives, I sidled past her cart on my way to anywhere but that hotel for a few hours.

Cole came in later that morning. After getting the dogs bedded and fed in the makeshift dog lot, we made our way back to the dive. Cole was well aware of the establishment's infamous reputation so she was less than excited when I told her where we were headed. However, after sleeping only a handful of hours during the previous week, and spending most of that time in minus temperatures, she was thankful to have a warm place to lie down.

In the room Cole wearily shed her layers of ice-covered clothing, but I—feeling less than confident with how I had left things with the maid—quickly poked my head next door to ensure she had put some toilet paper in. To my relief, she had.

In a sleep-deprived stupor, Cole ambled her way to the communal shower and through the wafer-thin wall I heard the water starting to run. At last, everything seemed to be going smoothly until I heard Cole shriek in terror.

I bounded out of our sorry excuse for a bed and ran into the darkness of the dingy bathroom. Immediately the lights came back on. I wasn't sure what kind of game was getting played so I asked Cole if she was OK.

"Ye-yeah. I'm fine. But the lights went out suddenly."

After surveying the scene and seeing no one and nothing nefarious, I stood very still while trying to piece it all together. The lights went out again. I spun around; they came back on. It took me a few seconds, but I realized they were on a timed motion sensor and someone needed to be moving in the center of the room to keep them on. Cole couldn't trigger them from behind the flimsy shower curtain.

The hotel staff may not have been the picture of professionalism, but apparently they gave a damn about their utility bills. I'd love to say we had a good laugh about it, but Cole, between her full-body fatigue and now jangled nerves, found no humor in the situation. She finished up and wearily wandered back to our room where we both crashed for several hours and tried to forget our boarding bad dream.

Meanwhile, Cole's Uncle David, a kindly, white-bearded, Oregonian, had flown in—along with Cole's mom and dad—to see the finish. They were all staying in what by Nome standards equated to five-star accommodations. They'd managed to book a room at a posh bed-and-breakfast run by a former mayor of Nome and his wife.

The place didn't allow mushers or dogs, but we joined them for breakfast a couple of mornings and the homey establishment embodied everything ours did not. There always seemed to be the tantalizing sounds of bacon sizzling and the heavenly scent of from-scratch blueberry pancakes coming from the kitchen. The owners prided themselves on being polite and courteous. And the accommodations were clean to the point of bordering on sterile, and on every wall hung dozens of awe-inspiring original paintings and museum-quality works of art depicting life in the north. This place was more welcoming than most visitor centers I've been in.

Despite Cole's relatives' luxurious lodgings, their stay also did not end in a picturesque way. Uncle David had eaten something on the flight up that didn't agree with him, and after a day or two, what started as a sour stomach developed into full-blown food poisoning. He missed a lot of the postrace festivities due to acute gut pain and near-constant diarrhea, but his living situation really took a turn for the worse when his ailment amplified to vomiting several times a day.

Early one morning, the man of the house was apparently on the porcelain throne, reading his morning paper, when Uncle David felt a nauseous wave wash over him. Doubled over in pain and knowing his internal plumbing was about to back up, he stumbled to the only bathroom in the establishment and began frantically pounding on the door, pleading with the B&B owner to let him in. God only knows what the poor pooping bastard was thinking as he kept shouting "Occupied!" and angrily instructing Uncle David to "Hang on a minute!"

Apparently there was no postponing this puke for even a few seconds, and in an act of desperation, Uncle David burst through the unlocked bathroom door and regurgitated all over the former mayor still sitting on the toilet with his pants around his ankles.

Needless to say, the two men didn't make much eye contact for the remainder of the time Cole's family stayed there, which ended up being not long due to these aforementioned circumstances. And, while the Iditarod left an indelible mark on all our memories, I think Cole's uncle may have, himself, left a lasting impression with at least one Nome resident.

And all of these misadventures made an impact on Cole and me, too. On the surface, owning forty sled dogs would suggest that the most vivid memories are made crossing finishing lines and soaking in race success.

But in our experience, getting to and from competitive events offers an equal number of obstacles to overcome.

While we toiled through many stressful setbacks—far too many—and endured countless embarrassments and awkward interactions, these engagements are part and parcel of the canine commitment. If we didn't own so many huskies and choose to race them, we never would have found ourselves in any of these situations in the first place. Our lives and our memories are all the richer for having survived so much suffering. It's really what being a kennel owner boils down to.

At its core, at its esoteric essence, at its bare-bones truth, owning forty dogs means having to contend with a never-ending succession of shit storms. It's a dog-eat-dog pursuit, and the people who last the longest are the ones who acknowledge this reality and accept there is no circumventing Murphy's Law, only enduring it. As such, I've embraced this edict: whatever doesn't kill you eventually makes a killer cocktail-party story.

Epilogue

WELL, THIS LITERARY JOURNEY IS NEAR ITS END AND A LOT has changed since some of these stories made their way from my cranium, to my computer, and ultimately to a reading audience. The book has come a long way—much as the kennel has since its ignoble inception.

I've talked to parents with grown children who've told me that no matter how old their kids get, when they look at them, they still see through them to the innocent infant they once were, toothless and drooling, speechless and cooing, and tripping over their own legs every time they attempted to stand on their own two feet. In some ways the kennel is like that for me. Despite our accomplishments, I will always hold dear the memories of when the dogs were an undisciplined mob of unruly pups, and the days when Cole and I excitedly sketched what we hoped would be better team configurations on napkins, and those embarrassingly honest years before we even owned a dog truck and would drive to and from races with all the dogs riding in our economy-sized vehicle, looking like the clown car at the circus when we unloaded everyone.

From these humble beginnings great things arose; the stories you just read are proof of that, but eventually all books must come to an end, much as the kennel itself is creeping closer to its terminus each passing year.

Since their stories were told in these pages, some of the dogs have passed away from old age, while others are in their golden years and long retired from running. They now spend their days snuggling on the couch or nestling into the poofy dog bed in front of the woodstove. Based on how long in the tooth a few have become, we never know just how much longer we will have with them before their spirits run off to join the ever-growing pack in the sky.

It's been hard saying good-bye—in general, but also over and over again—and witnessing these furry friends growing old in general, and not because senior dogs don't have their own deeply enjoyable personalities and endearing quirks. Sure, we wake up to puddles on the floor, we have to physically carry the dogs outside to poop, and at times even carry the water bowl to them because they are too frail to walk over for a drink without falling over or collapsing into it in an undignified and dangerous manner. I love my dogs, right up to their last minutes and beyond, no matter how decrepit they become or how much doting they need in their final days, hours, and minutes. I love them in the way they love me: unconditionally.

No, the difficult part is observing the physical decline and slowing down of personalities that for years didn't just seem invincible, they actually were somewhat indomitable. Dogs that grew stronger and more tireless the more miles we threw at them, and who showed more determination and raw will than any human or other animal I have ever known. My dogs were in many ways my heroes, and I've come to understand there's a reason why in comic books, Superman still looks the same today as he did back in the 1930s. Our heroes shouldn't age, get older, or weaker. We forever want to see them as they were in their prime, and so that has been the hardest part—watching dogs that were seemingly indestructible gradually change with age, slowly deteriorate over time, and eventually crumble under the weight of their advanced years.

Giving our dogs a home for their entire lives, we are capped by limits on our time and money. Not wanting to stretch these resources beyond forty dogs, we've made the decision to discontinue breeding and to stop adopting animals from the pound, and this has been a tough choice. We've earnestly worked to get the dogs to the physical and mental skill level they are at—able to break trail *for hours* on terrain they've never been on before, and meticulously listen to voice commands in order to achieve this task. This level of conditioning and aptitude took years to develop in them, and since experienced, knowledgeable dogs are better at teaching new and novice dogs than we are when starting their education from scratch, retiring now feels comparable to building your dream home, staying briefly, then moving out and monitoring your life's work as it dilapidates by degrees. It's a difficult and painful process to accept and witness.

Still, in terms of all the dogs we've shared so much of our adult lives with, it's like the old cliché goes: I would rather have loved and lost them, than never have known those dogs at all.

Also, in some ways, we may have retired from competitive mushing at just the right time. We had initially planned to take only one year off from racing for Lynx's birth and then get back on the runners. We deliberately chose to have our daughter while the dogs were still at their peak due to our desire for her to grow up in, and be a part of, the kennel we had built for more than a decade before she was born. But, Mother Nature had other plans.

While some—myself included—call it climate change (which happens four to five times more noticeably nearer the poles than the equator), and others believe the Earth is just experiencing a natural warming pattern, the bottom line for us was experiencing three non-winters in a row. In cold-weather months when we normally would be breaking trail in a slow slog through feet of snow, we experienced instead, in the final few years our dogs were still able-bodied enough to race, rain almost all winter long, trails filled with water, and lakes that didn't freeze. Competitive mushers had to pack up their operations and travel hundreds of miles north to eke out enough training, often at great expense due to the gas mileage and hotel costs racked up by living so far from home. We weren't interested in chasing snow across the state with a newborn, so rather than going out of competitive mushing with a bang, Cole's career ended in more of a fizzle (or perhaps splash is even more appropriate).

That being said, our final years with the dogs became much more enjoyable because we were not so hyper-focused on training to win. Every year that we raced, we witnessed how the competition incrementally pushed harder and harder each winter. When Cole first started racing, she was winning races with conditioning runs no longer than thirty miles and always training by sled. By the time she finished her final Iditarod in twenty-first place, she had been putting in two fifty- to sixty-mile runs a day and was one of the only people we knew not utilizing a snowmachine or other motorized vehicle in order to run excessively large strings of dogs.

I shudder to think of what teams presently trying to win are putting in for mileage these days, but I know for certain, my dogs and I would never want to partake in that much mind-bending time exercising. Too much of even a good thing is still too much.

For us, mushing was always about the overall journey, not solely the end goal of winning a race or crossing a finish line. We had always longed for adventures, and in lieu of racing we had more opportunities for them. We spent the remaining years with the dogs in their prime taking out sleds (when we could) for enjoyable runs exploring new trail and teaching Lynx the basics of mushing, and it was immensely satisfying for all of us.

Despite our kennel's early retirement from racing, I never lost the zest for mushing. I still love running dogs as much as the first time I took a team and sled out. It's just as fun, exhilarating, and rewarding as it ever was.

Perhaps that is why I am filled with an immense sense of dread for the eventual day that will come when there aren't enough dogs to make even a small team, or eventually, one at all. I know I will ultimately be left standing alone in the same spot where once so many canine bodies moved in a blur of motion, and hearing only the sound of silence where once so many huskies' voices howled in a unanimous chorus. It will be a surreal setting, and one I'm sure will fill me with forlorn feelings after so many years with so many dogs. They have been a superlative security system, explosively barking at any intruders—from scampering field mice to someone they don't recognize strolling up the driveway. They've provided heaping mounds of manure, converted to rich compost for my garden, and I'm not looking forward to procuring potting soil from outside sources. The exercise to keep them trained, cleaned, and fed has been a better workout than I could ever get at a gym, which is why I haven't stepped foot in one in twenty years. And of course, they've been constant and invaluable companions to my immediate family, visiting friends, and extended family, and hundreds of tourists to the kennel.

I will always be grateful to the dogs for the many things they have taught me, not the least of which is that every day with them brings a new story to tell. No matter how long I've known an individual, or the pack as a whole, they still surprise me, show me some new facet of their personality I've never seen, or teach me a concept I'd never considered. It's always felt as though when one chapter seemed to be coming to an end, another suddenly, unexpectedly, and eagerly began. So while this book may be at its conclusion, I am confident that there are many more adventures waiting for us and the dogs, on the trail of life we travel together. And whatever direction we go, I know I will hold dear the truth that I've felt great happiness *for* the dogs, I've experienced immense happiness *because* of the dogs, and as long as they are in my life, I will sincerely appreciate happiness *with* my dogs.

CPSIA information can be obtained
at www.ICGtesting.com
Printed in the USA
BVOW11s0550200217
476564BV00002B/2/P